MW01196620

The Book of Elven Magick:

The Philosophy and Enchantments
of the Seelie Elves, Volume 2

By The Silver Elves

ISBN-13: 978-1478157526

ISBN-10: 1478157526

Printed in the United States of America by CreateSpace

DEDICATION:

This book is dedicated to Vivienne Feorynsa Godwin, our beloved sister who founded the Elven Sisterhood.

TABLE OF CONTENTS

PART TWO:
DIRECTIONS AND DIMENSIONS IN MAGIC

Authors Note: A Word About Pronouns

The English language does not have a pronoun that covers both male and female in instances when it could be either. For instance, if we wrote, "The magician did the magic and then left his or her magic circle", this would be correct English, but this "his or her", or "his/her", seems cumbersome to us. Most people write, "The magician did the magic and then left their magic circle." This creates incorrect correlation between singular and plural, but is common usage. We have instead settled upon the use of "hir" which combines his and her, and sHe or SHe that combines she and he as an alternative.

Part One:
The Colors of Magic

CHAPTER 1:

RED MAGIC

Red Magic is the magic of sex, love, companionship and alliances. While many people believe the root of its power is passion and lust, the true source of empowerment for the red magic is natural affection and inclination towards kinship. Passion and lust are wild horses that one learns to ride, guide and master so that they can be utilized towards the realization and fulfillment of One's Will. Friendship, as always, is the underlying basis of all elven relationships.

After the elfin magician has completed the purple magic and actualized hir individual creative being and magic, sHe begins (usually) to seek other unique individuals with whom sHe can share the wonders of enlightened awareness and increase all of their powers through alliance and coordinated activity. This is not to say that sHe has not been seeking companions all along. This magic is so profound and so essential to the elven psyche that most of us are ever seeking companions, just as we are ever seeking the fulfillment of our creative impulses. However, in having accomplished, that is performed/created the prior magics spoken of in volume 1, the elfin mage is now in a better position to attract those who are truly right for hir, in union with whom sHe can achieve great things.

If we reverse the order in which we do these magics, which is often the case, where the people involved have, as yet, not realized their unique individuality, and get together due to their lack of personal strength, the relationship is usually doomed to failure. Even if the couple stays together they simply reinforce each other's misery and serve to heighten each one's personal weaknesses instead of overcoming them and replacing them with strength. The only truly secure relationships, from an elven point of view, are those among strong individuals who have realized their unique natures. This development of the individual in harmony with hir others is one of the primary goals of elven society.

The same is true of groups as well as the traditional romantic pair-bond. The group, in which there is one strong leader and a group of non-individual, and thus weak, followers is at its very heart an inadequate alliance. It is a chain with weak links and a strong clasp. On the other hand, a group that has a strong leader with a strong team of individuals, each with hir unique abilities and talents, is by far and away a more effective, efficient and powerful alliance.

The red magic is the magic for attracting such individuals for both romantic and other purposes, such as doing magic, and for securing the union in a way that will be lasting and fulfilling for all concerned. Relationships that are not satisfying to all involved never last (at least among elves where one is always free to come and go) and if they do endure they fail to generate the ecstatic energy, the loving, affectionate vibe that is so vital to our magic, in fact, to all magic. Ecstasy being a key to shamanic revelation.

But the object is not simply, as some people think, to fulfill one's lust (a bit of magic that produces temporary benefits and can carry with it potentially devastating consequences) but to find the right individuals with whom one can achieve all one's goals and desires. Which is not to say we elves are utterly against wild lustful sex with someone we just met as long as safe sex and due respect is involved; but wild sex, while great, is not the source of the enduring power into which this magic seeks to tap. Passing sexual relationships are like a sudden thunderstorm, potentially beautiful but quickly passing. In this magic we seek the Sacred Pool itself, the source of the magic.

People are like different elements of the periodic table. The combination of these different elements in various arrangements produces differing results. Some are explosive, some poisonous, some simply do not interact, are neutralizing for each other, or do very little of value and some combinations produce new, interesting and valuable molecules that are useful and productive. Finding the right people and aligning them correctly is the goal of the red magic.

The Dominating, "enculturating" forces and their servants are dedicated to creating masses of uniformed people who slavishly and mindlessly serve and praise the all-magnificent One. They constantly strive to create paranoia and prejudice so that individuals will never feel free to unite with each other, but will only feel safe cleaving to and obeying the All-Protector. This tendency to create social adhesion and a sense of protection of society's inhabitants is a natural and good thing. However, Dominator societies are like bodies whose immune systems turn upon their own selves, constantly perceiving those of its people who don't absolutely adhere to its ideas, social values, and fashions as enemies that must be eliminated. The basic impulse that drives such societies is good, but they are out of balance.

In contrast to Dominator societies that ever seek to expand, Seelie Elves are generally small group oriented individuals. We are tribal by nature and have come to understand consensus as the most effective means for group decision-making. Including the decision to appoint a team leader or director for this or that project. The goal of the Seelie Elf is to create small independent groups that foster individuality and simultaneously respect group differences.

The bureaucracy of the powers of domination seek to overcome individual and group conflict through force, by forcefully creating one large group in which there are no or few differences allowed. The Seelie Elves strive to overcome individual conflict by recognizing and fostering respect for individuality and promoting the right to disagree while nurturing compromise and consensus rather than force and violence as the means for resolving differences. Thus the Red

Magic is also the magic for creating and drawing together the members of one's coven, temple, vortex, etc. Note that in the fifth sub-race of the fifth root race (for more on this study Theosophy and Alice Bailey's Blue Books) the theme of the fourth ray was harmony through conflict, a Piscean Age idea. Now, as we move into the sixth sub-race, thus the Aquarian Age, the theme for the fourth (creative and harmonizing ray) is Harmony Through Diversity.

Yet, you will never find a Seelie Elf group that has one strong leader and a group of followers. While perhaps some members will be more experienced in magic than others, you will never find one all knowing authority. A true Seelie Elf would never create such a situation, and Seelie Elves would never tolerate it. Always, the Seelie vortex/coven will be a temporary and fluctuating gathering of miscellaneous magicians, held together primarily by their love of being together and the excitement that their gathering and interaction create, as well as their devotion to a shared Vision and Dream.

You will never find an exclusive Seelie Elf group in which members are sworn to be members for life, or to be members of that group and no other. Nor will you find a Seelie Elf coven that makes it difficult to get in. Seelie Elves are always easy going folk who have an immediate recognition of each other. Those who don't belong in a Seelie Elf vortex simply never feel comfortable around the Seelie Elves and soon leave of their own accord. Nor do we attempt to keep individuals against their will. While we may express how much we love them and will miss them, their will is foremost, and if they really wish to leave they always have our blessings in doing so. Our hope for such kin is only that they will leave with love and know that they are ever welcome among us.

It is, of course, natural that there is an affectionate overtone to Seelie Elf groups. While there may or may not be affairs among the various members, there is always a tendency to flirt, touch and, in general, exude sexuality around each other. Seelie Elves tend to be sensual people. We are excited by each other and constantly stimulated by our interactions. It is only natural that personal affairs develop under these circumstances.

The Domineering groups nearly always repress sexuality because sex brings individuals closer together and helps them form a commitment to each other, instead of to the mass, and thus the "One Leader/God", the "Cause", etc. That this causes neurosis, psychosis, is a small price to pay (in their minds) for a chance to control everyone and get to play God. In instances where sex is used as a controlling element in dominator cults, the groupings are always directed by the central leader who determines who should sleep with whom, thus continuing to exert hir control even in personal interactions. While Seelie Elves might put up with someone telling us whom we should sleep with, we would never endure being told we couldn't sleep with someone we love who returns our affection. Sexual coercion is not a part of the Seelie Elf culture. Free Love however ...

The Modus Operandi of the Dominating Mob is to keep people afraid, weak and ignorant. This tends to create a relatively stable but stagnate society. The amount that each culture is progressive and evolutionary can be directly equated to the degree of tolerance it shows its eccentric, mutant, Seelie, otherkin, Otherkind minorities. That is why Seelie Elf societies are seldom composed merely of elves. We attract elves, pixies, brownies, gnomes and all manner of folk to our world and all who come in sincerity are welcome.

The Wand

The first tool of the Red Magic is the Wand, which is related to the magical element/state of fire/radiance, the principle of will power, and obviously, the symbolic representation of the masculine aspect, the phallus, and the masculine within the feminine, the clitoris. That the clitoris is less obvious and hidden is in keeping with the fact that the feminine or yin aspect of will power achieves its will by circuitous and indirect means, often acting behind the scenes or through others, which is a very elfin form of magic.

The wand is also related in essence to the wizard's staff, the enchanter's cane, the shaman's bone (usually a finger bone), the witch's broom, the sorcerer's stick, the medicine man's feather, and the writer/ conjuror's pen/quill.

Wands can be made of any material, however, we suggest that ones that the magician makes or adapts hirs'elf are better/more powerful and magically vibrant, than those that are purchased. Particularly those that are commonly seen around these days of glass and crystal that are so fragile that their use as a magical tool is extremely limited (there are, naturally, exceptions to this. Note that for very delicate magics, such delicate tools may serve very well for it reminds us to be very cautious as we create out magic). As ever, unique is preferable to the common in most instances.

Since one's wand is an extension of one's phallic power (this is true whether the magician is male or female), it can be anointed with one's personal sexual fluids to make it attuned to one's essence, one's pro-creative s'Elfhood. Note that being a phallic energy, it reaches out to connect. It is an electric rather than magnetic power. It is extraverted, rather than introverted. It extends one's power. It channels one's energy. In some ways, it could be compared to an extension cord, as it extends the range of your power. Although, in other ways it can be likened to a battery, since it also stores up power to be used to start up your magic.

The wand is the tool most often associated with magicians and wizards (via Harry Potter) and thus it also contains the power of magical association, a type of sympathetic magic, since even those who don't believe in magic, still know that the wand is the tool of the magician.

There is, however, also the image of the faery princess wand, or the faerie godmother wand (the glass crystal wands are a good example of this type). For a number of years, these elves taught classes at a California state university. One of the things we would do in these classes was have a session in wand making. These were psychology classes so Zardoa would give a talk connecting magic, using popular books and movies on the subject, such as Harry Potter books, *Lord of the Rings*, etc. and relate the ideas of magic to the concepts of psychology that the students were studying to make these ideas more accessible to them.

We would bring in bags of sticks and small branches we'd found in the woods (since these classes usually had between twenty to thirty students, we collected these sticks for months so we'd have more than enough for each of them since we wanted them to have a choice). We also provided ribbon, hot glue, wire, colored markers for putting on runes or glyphs, and boxes of trinkets, old jewelry, or anything we thought might go into making a wand. We'd put these sticks in the middle of the classroom and in every case some students would rush out to grab the one they'd already chosen in their minds. They could, of course, use whatever was available and make it anyway they desired. In the long run, however, we found the males made some version of the Harry Potter or traditional magic wand, and the females almost always made some version of the faerie princess/ faerie godmother wand.

The Cup

The cup or chalice is the sacred symbol of communion. It has an affinity to the element/state of water/liquid and water, wine, etc. represent the fluids of life, both sanguine and seminal. When the magician drinks of the cup of hir true love's life, the magician imbibes hir love's very essence. (Read Nicholas DeVere's *The Dragon Legacy* for more on this. Although we should point out that DeVere's overall philosophy is basically an Unseelie point of view.)

The Christians use wine or grape juice, which is symbolic of wine, and these are mystically transformed into the Blood of Christ. They also mystically eat his flesh. However, we Seelie elves are not inclined toward cannibalism, even metaphoric or symbolic cannibalism, and prefer instead to drink both the actual and symbolic pro-creative juices of our adored ones, our divine partners and lovers, the fluid of sexual arousal and life.

Most Christians, no doubt, will think our symbolic and actual drinking of sexual fluids just as obscene as we find their drinking of blood and eating of flesh. Actually, probably more so, since in some instances where each volunteers hir blood and to the extent it does hir no harm, we see no problem with drinking of blood either. Still, we tend to prefer the sexual. The drinking of blood is associated with the Vampire mythos, and the eating of flesh is associated with ghouls and revenants. Vampires are usually associated with the Unseelie, as are revenants. We consider most vampires to be distant cousins (again read DeVere's *Dragon Legacy* and Laurence Gardner's the Realm of the Ring Lords for more on this.)

Traditionally, in Witchcraft the insertion of the athame (knife) into the cup was symbolic of the act of intercourse. However, for we Seelie Elves, the insertion of the knife into the cup is a symbol of rape. For us, the wand being plunged into the cup is symbolic of consenting intercourse, which is the only type we engage in. Rape is dark magic and leads to terrible karma for the violator as well as continual trauma for the violated. In fact, we would say that most dark magics, the magics of domination are a form of rape, usually of a psychic and psychological variety.

A chalice should be relatively easy to obtain. You may wish to inscribe or paint your personal symbols around it. Making your own is always preferable, but how many of us are in a position to take a class in pottery and craft our own chalice? However, most of us, if we are unable to do this, are able to find hand made pottery cups or chalices that are individual rather than mass produced. Still, any cup will do at need, and you can paint or inscribe your personal glyphs on it, and add decorative elements to make it magical. Zardoa's personal cup is a unique, one of a kind, glazed chalice. Elantari, also known to us as Her Majesty, obtained a metal goblet on which she engraved runes. The more individual and unique we make it, the better as far as these elves are concerned.

The chalice is a particularly feminine symbol, and is associated with the vagina; however, it is indicative of the receptive aspect in all of us. If the wand is the play, the chalice is the audience. If the wand is Halloween candy, the chalice is the bag to collect it in. It symbolizes our capacity for helping, assisting, encouraging, and also accepting and receiving. Is it better to give or receive? The Seelie elf says it is best to give and to receive creating a cycle of balanced reciprocation. In this way the magic ever flows. And surely that is one of the goals of elfin magic, to create magic that continually radiates, that ever flows from the source constantly nurturing us and our others and illuminating our lives. The chalice of Elfin Magic is a cup that is ever overflowing, a fountain of healing waters pouring forth unto the world.

The power of the wand is useless if there is no chalice with which to receive the benefits you have willed to be. The phallus vainly humps the air without the hand or vagina to "cup" it. One may evoke the abundance of nature but if one cannot receive it, what good is it to them? Doing magic merely for the sake of others is like feeding others but never feeding ones'elf. It is an unbalanced situation that cannot endure. The wand and cup go together and are meant to work in concert, each fulfilling its part in the magic of creating ecstasy.

The Robe

The third tool of the Red Magic is the Robe or garment/raiment. It is associated with the element/state of air/gaseous because in this case its use is particularly ornamental and is meant for its visual and thus fantasy/imaginative arousing properties. Therefore the magical garments of the red magic are best when they are erotically and sexually suggestive as well as evocative of the magic. After all, the purpose of the red magic is to arouse and successfully channel the sexual energy, to create an atmosphere of attraction to draw to the magician the individuals who are most attuned to fulfilling hir will and hir destiny.

It would be difficult for most of us to make our own sexy clothes, so in this case the emphasis is not on a unique or individually created magical tool, but on "hot" and alluring. However, like other instances when one may not necessarily be able to make our own magical tool, the creativity comes from putting it together in a new way, from making it our own, adding our individual runes, sigils, glyphs, or symbols to it. At the same time you want to look really good, not corny. You want it to evoke sexuality in a truly magical, and elven/faerie, way. This is true even if you are performing the ritual alone (which some shy elves might prefer), for it is not for the mundane world that we do our magic, but for the spirit world that is the foundation of the material world.

This is one of the few cases where imitation for most individuals is often more successful than being entirely original. That is if the individual magician doesn't have a clear idea of what constitutes sexy, sHe could take her cues from movies or other forms of media. Often television and movies get magic very wrong, or don't really get it at all, or exaggerate it to the point of ridiculousness, but fashion and presentation is their field. That is the area of magic where they truly are experts. They know sexy and they know how to make the vibrations, the ritual, resonate with power. (Note there are also sites on the Internet that cater to the Sexy Witch.)

The point is to be as sexy as possible any way the enchanter can manage it. However, the idea is not to be simply sexy, but to make one's magical garments sexually alluring, to be the sexy witch, wizard, enchanter, magician, sorceress. (See our dear friend and elfin sister LaSara Firefox's book, *Sexy Witch*.)

The Talisman/Spirit Sigil

The Talisman/Spirit Sigil is a disk with the spirit's insignia/signature inscribed upon it. It is related to the earth/solid element/state since it is intended as a house/receptacle for the designated spirit. It is also meant to help materialize something, in this case, to manifest one or more individuals into the magician's life, since we are using this in the Red Magic, the magic of relationship.

Upon the talisman you may paint or inscribe the name of a spirit, or for instance, your desired love; or some symbol, representing your desire. You could also take a talisman you have purchased and carry it with you during the magic ceremony, instilling it with your purpose and will, and the vibration of the magic you evoke. After the circle you may wish to wear it about with you radiating its vibrations wherever you go. You could also give it to someone as a present, or plant it strategically in some crucial "crossroads" where its powers would be most productive, and those you seek to draw to you are most likely to pass.

Just as a reminder, trying to force someone into a relationship with you who is not really attracted to you is magic that accrues loads of unpleasant karma and seldom works out well for the magician except as a lesson in what not to do. The Red Magic is not a magic of force, it is a magic of enchantment, charm and persuasion. In doing magic to attract a particular person to you it is wise to add a clause stating that you only want this particular person if it is beneficial to both of you, and if this person isn't the right one for you that sHe should serve as a image/model for the type of person you are doing the magic to attract. In other words, if you can't have hir, you are telling the spirits to attract someone like hir, only better.

Also, in Elven magic, it is good to remember that the basis of all elven relationships is friendship. Friendship is first and foremost to elves, for from friendship all opportunities flow. It is from friendship that business opportunities stem, romantic opportunities arise, learning opportunities develop, and, to the elven mind, everything else worth having. Without the underlying basis of friendship, every relationship turns to dust.

Still, it is not wrong to desire a particular person, nor to use the magic to attract them, or attempt to persuade them of the benefits of association. But it is wise to formulate one's magic in such a way that if the person you do desire is not a good fit, so to speak, the magic will attract the one (or ones) that is right for you. However in the long run, this magic is not so much about attracting a particular person or persons, but about developing your powers of enchantment. This is the magic of the Ganconer, the Love Talker, or the Love Whisperer. (See the movie *About Adam*, starting Stuart Townsend, which is about a Ganconer. Also see the *Tao of Steve* starring Donal Logue, which is about a Ganconer who is not quite as developed as the one in About Adam.)

Red Magic Ceremony

White magic – clean and purify the temple/shrine/sanctuary – cleanse your body – purify your mind.

Black magic – secure the circle. Keep your silence, let only those participating know where and when. Be sure you have your prophylactics.

Green magic – create a healing atmosphere, project positive energy into the circle, be charming, happy, relaxed, but ever aware of your purpose and goals. Be sure to have your lubricants.

Orange magic – have the tools set up, whatever you may need. The red magic ceremony is a "date" with the spirit. Have what you need to have a good time but always sincerity is more powerful than superficial pretense and display.

Purple magic – be creative, improvise, use the ceremony below but change it to your needs, add to it, make it your own, or make your own. Remember the magics in this book, and in volume one, are only guidelines meant to inspire you. Making the magic your own means altering the ceremony, incantations and tools as circumstances and need demands, as well as adding your own style, your own flavor to the magic. Remember, it is your magic.

At the same time, while sincerity is most important, drama is a traditional and powerful means of raising power, of creating the atmosphere of the magic, of making the magic feel alive. This is particularly true when others are participating in the ceremony/rite. As we've pointed out previously, watching television shows or movies that have magic rituals is often a good way to get a sense of how to empower a ritual; and while some folks can read from a book, such as this, and read well in an impromptu fashion, most people tend to stumble when they first read something and are unaware of where emphasis should be placed or how the language flows. Therefore, as with theatre, practice, rehearsals and read-throughs help. Read-throughs of the ritual ahead of time can familiarize the participants with what they will be reading and give them time to develop a sense of power in their speech to lend to their performance. And magical rituals are performances. It is not an accident that theatre, initiation rituals, and religion all originate from magic and shamanism. (Read the introduction to Frazer's *The Golden Bough*.)

Remember magic is primarily a language of symbols, as dreams are. However, these symbols are not merely communicated via glyphs, and sigils, which in many ways are linked to left brain linear activity. Magic seeks to engage the right brain. Symbols are not composed simply of signs, or magical words (such as using Arvyndase [see our book *Arvyndase (SilverSpeech): A short course in the magical language of the Silver Elves*), but also by using magic ritual/play with its smells and drama. Drama is the main symbol. The atmosphere/ambience of the magic is symbolic. Magic ritual is a play made to communicate to and entertain the spirits. If they like our play they will be more inclined to help in fulfilling our wishes. Make your magic dramatic, exciting, inspiring, interesting and powerful. Put your heart into. Put your soul into it. It is your magic, make it your own just aa various actors and theatre companies make Shakespeare's plays their own by performing them in their own unique way.

The double circle can have Enki to the south, Avalae to the West, Alavarfyn to the North, and Welolynver to the East. Between those names write the names of those you desire, either real or fantasy, movie star, rock star or girl/boy next door. Remember, what we are seeking is not necessarily that person, but someone similar to the qualities that this person(s) exemplifies. If you have a group in mind and a lot of names, you might wish to use initials. You can also use images from magazines, etc.:

"AWAKEN, OH, MIGHTY ONES, ANCIENT POWER OF THE EARTH AND STARS, LISTEN TO US, YOUR KINDRED, WHO THIS NIGHT CALL TO YOU THAT OUR FRASORITY (FELLOWSHIP) OF LONG AGO BE REMEMBERED STILL AND THAT YOU WITH US BE JOINED IN PURPOSE AND IN WILL. FOR WE WOULD THAT OUR LOVERS TRUE, WHEREVER THEY MIGHT BE, DO COME TO US AND LEND THEIR AID TO OUR STRUGGLE TO BE FREE AND UNITED SO, WE MIGHT TOGETHER KNOW THAT LOVE OF ECSTASY'S CARESS AND

THAT THIS SACRED UNION IN YOUR EYES WILL BE BLESSED.

"COME TO ME, MY LOVERS, COME TO ME, MY FRIENDS, COME TO ME, COMPANIONS, ON THE STARLIT PATH OF MAGIC. COME TO ME, LET US BE AS ONE, DO NOT HESITATE. COME, COME, COME. LET US BE AS ONE. COME TOGETHER, COME IN JOY. LET US UNITE BENEATH THE BRIGHT MOONLIGHT ON THE PATHWAY TO DELIGHT. COME, MAGIC KINDRED. COME TO ME THIS NIGHT THAT WE MIGHT STRUGGLE ONWARD TOWARD THE DAWNING LIGHT WHEN LOVE WILL REIGN UNHINDERED FOR ALL THE WORLD TO SEE AND WE SHALL LIVE FOREVER IN TRUTH AND ECSTASY.

"FROM THE FAR REACHES OF THE GALAXY, FROM THE VERY EDGE OF SPACE, DEAR LOVER, WON'T YOU COME TO ME SO LOVING WE'LL EMBRACE. NO MATTER WHAT THE DISTANCE, NO MATTER HOW LONG THE TIME, IN THIS OR FUTURE LIVES, TOGETHER WE WILL FIND EACH OTHER AND TOGETHER WE WILL CLIMB THE STAIRWAY TO HEAVEN, THE SPIRAL STAIRCASE OF THE MIND, THE SACRED PATH TO FAERIE THAT EVERY ELF MUST FIND.

"I CAN FEEL YOU NEAR ME. I CAN FEEL YOUR TOUCH. I CAN FEEL YOUR PANTING BREATH. I WANT YOU OH, SO MUCH. I KNOW YOU'RE GETTING CLOSER. FOR I CAN FEEL THE HEAT. MY EARS KEEP RESOUNDING WITH THE STEADY POUNDING BEAT OF YOUR HEART AS IT DRAWS CLOSER STILL, TO INTERTWINE WITH MINE FOR EVERY BREATH, LIKE FLOWERS FRAGRANCE FINE, AWAKENS ALL MY SENSES WITH PROMISES DIVINE. MY BODY DOES REJOICE AND SINGS A SONG OF MAGIC WITH ITS SECRET INNER VOICE."

(PICKING UP THE WAND.)

"To give is to receive, for in receiving do we give pleasure and in giving do we receive. Fill my cup with pleasure, with the sacred nectar of life and secret elixir of eternity that resides within our very being. I receive that I may give and give that I receive. Know this, this secret of life, all we give away comes back to us, and all to which we cling must be lost.

"Fill my cup with happiness that I might share, and in sharing have it truly. Fill my cup with love that in loving I may transform the world."

(Now take the wand and gently plunge it into and out of the cup and back again.)

"Giving is receiving and receiving I do give. Sharing is having, in sharing I do live. Together we do triumph over obstacles too great for each alone and thus united we do come to know our home is where the heart is, when those hearts in love unite and sharing we awaken with the world a light that shall lead us to the dawning of a new and vibrant day, and by our loving example demonstrate the way for those who are still searching, for those who do still care, for those who still with open hearts for the dawning do prepare. But let us not with artifice proceed from hence anon, for only in the purity of nature can truth be known."

(Remove the magical garments.)

"I STAND BEFORE YOU NAKED, TRUSTING AND UNARMED AND DO SWEAR BY MY VERY SOUL I SHALL DO YOU NO HARM. I DO SWEAR BY MY SPIRIT'S LIGHT THAT I SHALL EVER STRIVE TO TREAT YOU WITH LOVING CARE AS LONG AS I'M ALIVE. I DO SWEAR WITHIN MY MIND TO SPEAK NOT HARSHLY OR BE UNKIND AND BY MY BODY I DO SWEAR TO TREAT YOU ALWAYS WITH GENTLE CARE AND IF YOU DO SWEAR THE SAME TO ME THEN WE MAY LIVE IN ECSTASY AND JOY AND PLEASURE FOR ETERNITY.

"SO SHALL IT BE" 3X

(Now take the talisman and say, while you rub it against your body:)

"I DO EMPOWER THIS TALISMAN THAT IT WILL BE A BEACON TO DRAW TO ME MY DESTINED AND TRUE LOVERS SO TOGETHER WE WILL FIND THE WAY TO FULFILLMENT IN ECSTASY, LIBERATION IN UNION, AND TRUTH IN PARADOX. COME TO ME, MY HOLY ONES, MY SACRED LOVERS, MY ECSTATIC COMPANIONS. COME TO ME AND LET US IN LOVE BE TOGETHER FOREVER. THE FRICTION OF OUR BODIES SHALL LIGHT THE FIRE OF OUR SOULS AND BY ITS LIGHT THE TRUTH, OUR SPIRITS KNOW. AND THE HEAT THAT WE DO GENERATE WILL WARM A WORLD TURNED COLD AND GIVE US EACH THE COURAGE TO LIVE OUR LOVE SO BOLD THAT ALL MAY SEE IT AND SEEING THUS DO LEARN THAT THE ONLY LIFE WORTH LIVING IS ONE IN WHICH LOVE BURNS. RADIATE MY POWER, CALL TO ME THE FLOWERS, BRING ME MY DESIRE AND FILL MY LIFE WITH FIRE TO WARM MY VERY SOUL.

"COME TO ME, COME TO ME, COME TO ME AND IN COMING KNOW THAT WE SHALL IN LOVE FOREVER GROW. FOR LOVE THAT IS STATIC IS NO LOVE AT ALL, LOVE LIVES IN LOVING

AND THIS IS MY CALL. I SEND MY LOVE TO YOU, WHEREVER YOU MAY BE THAT MY LOVE MAY FREE YOU TO RETURN TO ME. AND THE POWER OF THIS MAGIC SHALL ETERNAL BE REBORN, LIKE A PHOENIX RISING FROM THE FLAMES ON THE BRILLIANCE OF THE MORN, OF PAST HEARTACHES FORGOTTEN, WE SHALL BE FOREVER SHORN, FOR A NEW LIFE EMERGES WITH THE RISING OF THE DAWNING OF OUR LOVE.

"AND NOW THAT I DO GO FORTH FROM THIS SACRED CIRCLE, SO SHALL THIS HOLY MAGIC BEGIN TO SPIRAL OUTWARD UNTIL IT TOUCHES EACH OF YOU FOR WHOM IT IS INTENDED AND DRAW YOU BY THE STRAIGHTEST ROUTE UNTIL WE ARE UNITED, AND THEN UNITED DO WHAT LOVERS DO ETERNAL, CREATING PARADISE BY OUR HEAT SUPERNAL, FOR THE SACREDNESS OF THE HOLY ARE ASCENDED FROM GREAT PASSION AND SO WE SHALL IN UNION BE ANGELS IN OUR FASHION AND IN FASHION EVER CHANGING ALWAYS BE IN STYLE, FOR OUR LOVE SHALL SET THE PACE AND WE SHALL SERVE AS MODELS FOR THE HUMAN RACE."

CHAPTER 2:

BLUE MAGIC

Blue Magic is the magic for the attainment of knowledge and wisdom. It is the magic of wizards, and the magic tools that are specific to it are the staff, the lamp, the book of shadows, and the shield.

A wizard, while very powerful, independent, and often hermit-like, is nonetheless, a community oriented person. A wizard always works for a community or a group of people, even when sHe works alone. An individual with wizardly powers, who does not work for, or within the context of a community, is called a sorcerer. (We do not mean to imply any negative connotation here to the term sorcerer, as is so often the case in many traditions. We simply are striving to differentiate a sorcerer from a wizard from a Seelie Elf viewpoint.)

With the Blue Magic, one attains knowledge, and not exclusively occult knowledge, but knowledge of the world in general, but also begins to develop the wisdom to use that knowledge/information/power, for the benefit of all. They say that this is the Information Age, which means this is truly the Age of Wizards and Blue Magic.

Once the wizard attains knowledge (which for a wizard is truly a never ending process and aspiration), what does sHe do with it? Again, we say, the wizard uses it wisely. In fact, you could say that an occult definition, or perhaps an elfin definition of a wizard, is someone who uses knowledge wisely. The wizard ever strives to create something magnificent for hir group and for humanity at large, to extend the boundaries of "human" knowledge, of intelligence, to demonstrate through excellence the means to a renewed future. These are the markings of a wizard.

It is significant that the blue magic comes after the red, since the wizard, while independent in his workings, is communal in his results and the effects of his creations. It is therefore understandable that communities support their wizards. Research wizards working under grants are a typical example. However, unfortunately these wizards are often encouraged to reach a designated result based on the desires of those who financially support them. This subordination of the wizard's power is an act of the dominating forces that seek to bribe the wizard into reinforcing the social and cultural mores rather than acting independently in the search for truth, which is the keynote of a true wizard, even when supported by others. This independence of research and the conclusions reached are vital to every true wizard.

It's no accident that the head of a Mafia family is called the "Godfather". The basic strategy of the G.O.D. crowd, the dominance cult, is to buy the wizards and their knowledge. Knowledge is power and power is always to be held, in their minds, by the few in order to control the many. The role of the true wizard is very difficult here because on the one hand he is faced with either bending to the will of the great power or being crushed (or in many cases, simply never get the funding needed to do hir research). It is a question of integrity. If the wizard accepts funding must sHe come up with the expected results, no matter what the truth? The elfin wizards typically accept just enough to continue their work without selling their souls.

Just as dangerous is the tendency for wizards to begin to feel alienated from the people because of hir special nature and to throw their lot in with the dominance crowd. Alas the Unseelie Elves also often seek to raise themselves above the common person because of their "special destiny" with no intention of lifting up those beneath them. They believe they are destined to rule by virtue of their superior nature. The Seelie Elves believe our superior nature gives us the responsibility to guide others so they will be capable of ruling their own s'elves.

36

It is the Seelie wizards' strategy to "sell out" just enough to have our works and knowledge integrated into domestic/domesticated society, so that it will be absorbed by the followers of the Domination Clique. We are not in opposition to traditional society, nor are we at war with G.O.D. in the way that the Dominators are at war with and wish to bend us to their will. We do not seek to overthrow the Dominators, but rather to enlighten him/them. We do not seek to destroy society but to uplift it, by infusing it with individual initiative and genius, and to find/arouse that genius in every person in whatever way they are able to develop and demonstrate it.

The goal of the Seelie elf wizard is ever to share knowledge, not for the purposes of controlling people, but to uplift the general state and level of intelligence in humanity. We are dedicated to the knowledge that true power resides not in its exclusive possession but in sharing it with as many minds as are capable of handling it. From our point of view, the more intellects we have working on any particular problem the greater our chances of finding a true solution.

Often the Seelie elf wizard is seen by society as the mad scientist, the eccentric inventor, or the daring entrepreneur who works on hir own in hir basement, garage, or cave (the shield) to invent/create something that alters the way things are done, that revolutionizes society. Seelie wizards are indeed geniuses, but then every elf has a bit of genius in hir.

Thus every Seelie elf is potentially a wizard. It is the destiny of every Seelie elf to know hirs'elf, hir true potential and genius and to fulfill it. For some Seelie elves, their genius, their wizardry, is to see, know, understand and foster the genius in others. These Seelie elves we call the Wizard Masters. Seelie elves who excel in many fields, we call Master Wizards.

(For young or newly aspiring wizards we recommend our friend Oberon Zell-Ravenheart's "Grimoire for the Apprentice Wizard".)

The Staff

The staff is a traditional wizard's tool. It is an extension of the wand, and like the wand it is associated with the element/state of fire/radiance. Since the staff is also like a cane, it has the added symbolism of being a tool for the aged, and thus hopefully, the wise. But the staff is also a martial weapon that allows the user to both strike and keep their opponents at a distance. Thus the staff symbolizes an increase in the range of one's effective powers.

As stated in volume 1, the staff is associated with the magical spear, the Spear of Lugh, the Spear of Destiny that pierced the Christ's side, and the Spear of Genghis Khan, all of which are symbolically the same spear. Note also the Spear of Odin and the Staff, which he is typically shown carrying, are really the same magical tool.

A staff can be made from the branch of a tree, or a bamboo shaft, or even a broom or a mop handle, etc. You could even make it of metal tubing, although in the case of the staff, we advise you to choose endurance and strength over fragile beauty. Your staff can be painted, inscribed, or decorated to your personal taste, magic, etc.

It is interesting that the word staff is also used to denote a group of assistants and colleagues that aide one in one's work, thus once again, we are reminded that the wizard does not act for hims'elf alone, nor does he always act by hims'elf, but often leads and directs a group or a team dedicated toward achieving a particular goal. Gandalf both in the Hobbit and the Lord of the Rings is a good example of this, so is Merlin in his role of nurturing and advising King Arthur and his Knights of the Round Table.

Staff was also an ancient building material combining plaster of Paris and hemp, thus we gain the idea that the task of the wizards is to construct something substantial. And the staff also indicates the lines upon which musical notation is written, the staff lines denoting different pitches, thus we have the idea of a systematic differentiation of tone designed to signify and thus add in the creation of music; it "maps" the interaction of notes in combinations that create melody, harmony, and dissonance. Thus to be a wizard often indicates the power to know at what vibration individuals resonate, and to combine them purposefully for achieving specific effects.

And finally, let us remember that bread or other staples of one's diet are referred to as the staff of life, telling us that the wizard feeds the basic needs of those sHe serves, giving them what they need to live truly and successfully. This last connotation is very important for it takes the spear, the item of war, back to the staff, an item of martial arts, to the staff, that is the wheat sheaf, the corn stalk, and the hoe used for farming and gardening, and therefore back from male dominated war cultures to feminine agricultural societies. (See the writings of Marija Gimbutas.)

Of course, before that there were the hunter-gatherer societies that also had the spear for hunting, and the staff in the form of a blow dart tube. So we are not trying to dispense of the idea of the staff/staff as a tool for combat, particularly in the case of magical combat, but to include with it the idea of nurturing and growing. Magic is never primarily about conflict. Magical combat (Black Magic, see volume 1) is sometimes necessary, but it is only important to secure the elven wizard/magician and hir circle so sHe may go on to the creative/higher magics.

Note also the Native American's coup stick, which is another form of the staff used in battle, but also used in practice for combat. Faerie battles were also often carried on in this way (rather like paintball really) with real strikes but few deaths or injuries. When Zardoa Silverstar, one of the authors of this book, was at military school, a Colonel from the Army who worked at the Pentagon, and was a veteran of WW2, would come to his school each Saturday to drill the battalion. In the afternoon, he would take them for a walk in the surrounding woods where some of the battles of the Civil War had taken place, divide the battalion into two groups that would eventually come together in a mock battle, with the two groups knocking each other down as they battled with wooden toy rifles. It was seldom that anyone got hurt, more than some sore fingers that had been whacked, but it was great fun and Zardoa and nearly everyone else there, grew to love it. It reminded him of Faerie Battles of long ago before the big folk came and actually wanted to kill us. Note the Irish game of hurling and the game of lacrosse as modern equivalents of ancient Faerie combat. (The rifle, by the way, is an extension of the bow and arrow, which is a derivation of the spear and the atlatl.)

Still, the primary use of the staff in elfin magic is one of using magic wisely, as well as, reaching a point where one directs others in magic. Thus the staff is a tool of the Master of Ceremonies, the one who directs the magic working. (In this form note its relation to the swagger stick, the Field Marshal's baton, the orchestra conductor's baton, and, in particular, the bandmaster's Mace.) It is also a walking stick, or climbing stick, thus it is connected to the Alpenstock used for climbing mountain paths. It is a tool for the old, wise wizard and in this way comes to be associated with longevity. Since elves are noted for our longevity, the staff is a particularly elfin magical tool.

The Book of Shadows

The Book of Shadows is a magical diary/journal of your thoughts, experiences, feelings, magical workings, dreams, successes and lack of success in magic. It contains the spells you've cast, the magic rituals and ceremonies you've performed, and the results thereof. It is associated with the element/state of water/liquid since it, like the cup, is a receptacle. It begins empty/blank and gets filled with your magic. Although some might associate it with air/gaseous since it is filled with thoughts, ideas and experiences. Make your own decision on this. The book of shadows is equivalent to a scientific journal of one's research and results. While it can be important to one personally, its greatest value is that it contains a record of one's magic that can be passed on to others who repeat or modify one's experiments. Although, honestly, these elves also just find them cool. A Book of Shadows is often a very beautiful thing even when it is quite simple. (Note: the leather covered binder that the brothers carry in the television show *Supernatural* that belonged to their father, which is filled with his experiences and research about demons, vampires, and other beings, is really and essentially a Book of Shadows.)

When we say results of our spells, these elves include not only whether the specific goal the magic was done for was obtained, but also the dreams we have after the working if they are relevant, and any sign, incident, or event that occurs within a week or two of the working that seems to have bearing upon it. Also, we may include the oracles we usually do after magic, and what they say to us about the power and potential success of our incantations, spells and conjurations. These signs may include nature signs, or even something someone says to us without even realizing they are relaying a message from the Spirit world.

Any blank book will do as a book of shadows, but you may wish to decorate the cover as well as the contents with your personal symbology. If you draw, draw in it, or take photos to put in it, or if you wish cut out pictures that you feel are appropriate to paste in. And while it will become increasingly enchanted as you use it, that is as you write and draw in it, you may also wish to cast a spell upon it before beginning its use, although after or during the process of decorating it with sigils, etc. And if you wish, these very spells may be the first things you write about when you begin bringing your Book of Shadows to life.

However, that it is a book of Shadows indicates that it is not the magic itself but a reflection or result of the magic. (Although, as we just said, it does have its own magic, but a receptive magic mostly, a container of spells. Plus any wards, bindings or other safeguards you may wish to cast upon it to keep it from prying eyes.) A book of shadows is often kept secret until far into the future. Oft times, there is much that is written between the lines. Some books of shadows are written in a runic script or code so that only those who know the script can decipher it. While nearly any code can be broken, a code that utilizes a particular book and gives references to page – paragraph, line and position of the word in the line is only decipherable if one knows which book is used as reference.

But a book of shadows is also so called because it deals with those aspects of life that are shadowy and not entirely pliable to empirical science. Like sociology and psychology and economics, magic sits on the corner of the fence that borders science, art and the unknown. The book of shadows deals not only with what is seen but what is unseen, what is felt, what is intuited. The book of shadows deals with those things that can only be seen in darkness such as the stars, thus sometimes we elves call it a Book of Starlight.

The book of shadows in another form is symbolic of your great work, the project that your wizardly s'elf is determined to accomplish. It contains the plans, notations and blueprints for its achievement. The tool for writing in the Book of Shadows is usually a pen, a form of the Wand. In a sense, writing or drawing in a Book of Shadows, in the minds of the elves, is itself a spell casting. It is a time binding magic linking the past, the future and the eternal present.

The Lamp

We consign the Lamp under the element/state of air/gas since it is a tool that is meant to illuminate the environment for the sake of the eye, the "vision" and thus the mind. Some might consign it to fire/radiance, but the tool is not the fire, but the lamp that holds the fire. Others might consign it to water/liquid because it often holds the oil, upon which the fire depends, or earth/solid, because the earth holds fire and water, but to these elves it is the oxygen that feeds the fire and the air that carries the light, so to speak, that signifies the significance of the lamp. Once again, use your own intuition when making attributions. Remember it is your own elven magic you are creating.

In the Tarot, the lamp is often carried by the Wizard (Hermit) along with hir staff, and in some cards sHe bears hir book of shadows under hir arm. But in reality, just as often, we find the lamp being carried by the acolyte who assists the wizard and acts as a member of his team/staff, just as a nurse hands instruments or holds a light for a surgeon. That someone fulfills an assisting role to a wizard should in no way be taken as demeaning to the individual, for each member of the team is vital to its success. To paraphrase a theatrical expression, there are no small roles, only petty egos. It should be noted that at the end of a film, everyone who participated in the making of the film, even the person who went for coffee is given due credit. Note that at the Academy Awards the winners spend a great deal of time thanking everyone involved with the project for its success.

The lamp is symbolic of the wizard's power to uplift us, enlighten us, to show us the way…to reveal the mysteries, the shadows, and the occult to us. And as such the lamp so symbolizes any other tool or devices or stratagems that the wizards might utilize for that purpose, including but certainly not exclusively, humor. The lamp lights our way through darkness. It represents knowledge and enlightenment. It symbolizes the spirit that motivates those higher and more evolved beings who reach out to uplift those of us searching for the truth in the dark of the world. It is the light in the forest we see when we are lost and our elven kindred find us and lead us home to safety. (If you feel lost in the world, don't worry, your elven kindred are coming for you. They are searching at this very moment. Why else has this book found its way into your hands?)

Any lamp will do, even a flashlight; however, the artistic aspect – the atmosphere or ambience of the magic – is best served by elegance than by strict utility. Remember, all magic tools are meant not simply to be functional, but to evoke a particular feeling when one uses them. Everything in a magic ceremony should resonate the feeling of magic, so that that feeling/emotion can be directed toward the success of the purpose for which the magic is being done.

Lamps can be acquired in garden stores, also in shops that have decorative furnishings. Often the lamp carries a candle, so the candle itself is an associative tool, and in a pinch a simple candle will do. We once had a Hindu monk give us a blessing and he had us take an old fashion brass lamp (the type typically shown as holding genies) we had on one of our shelves, fill it with cooking oil, and place a rolled up piece of cotton string soaked in the oil (caution: synthetic material will not do), and light it. This created a very ancient style oil lamp. A plate and a candle with a mirror behind it will work as well. You probably have other, and perhaps better, ideas that have already occurred to you.

The Shield

The shield is related to the element/state of earth/solid and is another form of the pantacle (seal of magic), coat of arms, etc. The shield might seem an unusual tool for a wizard but the simple fact is that greatness and excellence often inspires envy from the dark and frustrated victims of the Dominance syndrome. Remember, Satan is just G.O.D.'s alter ego. The dominance clique constantly enforces its rule through terror, and in order to have terror you must have ogres and demons who are terrifying.

The shield signifies the wizard's right and ability to defend hirs'elf. It also symbolizes the right of the wizard and hir people to create their own world, to think for thems'elves, set up their own rules of life, and to venture into spaces as yet uncharted. All of which requires not only daring but also caution and precautions. One of the simplest forms of the shield is invisibility, or anonymity. Its magic shields us from the unwanted prying of those who have no need or business looking into our lives. If no one knows of your existence, or of your magic, or what you are doing magically, they cannot interfere with, nor counter-act, your magical workings. Therefore sometimes, perhaps often, the greatest shield is the one that is not seen, like trees that keep a beautiful house from sight so no one knows it is there. However, if outsiders gain even a hint that something is going on they become intrigued, for secrecy puzzles them, in which case, open innocence is often the best face to put forward. Each must judge for hir own situation. Remember puzzles evoke the mysterious, and thus the great Mystery. In nearly every soul there is an eternal quest for the solution to the Great Mystery and little mysteries and puzzles arouse this primary instinct.

This does not mean that one has to hide their magic, or the fact that sHe is a wizard; however, one needs to be prepared for dealing with the nosey and the inquisitive. Of course, it is possible to be a wizard publicly without letting everyone see all your magic. Each must decide how much it is prudent to reveal.

Additionally, it should be noted that the wizard's shield is not for hirs'elf alone, but symbolizes the fact that the wizard is a guardian and protector of hir people. When one becomes a wizard, sHe in effect becomes a "parent/mentor" to developing Seelie elf spirits, either protecting and nurturing them, and/or serving as a living example of Seelie magic and culture.

A shield-bearer commonly carries the shield, that is, while the wizard goes about hir work, others on hir "staff" go about the task of defensive magic. Public relations officials are modern day equivalents of shield bearers.

You can make your shield of wood or metal, or any other substance that seems appropriate to you. The shield in this case is not necessarily one that actually needs to fend off swords. This is a magical shield, a symbol of the wards that protect your magic. Its power comes not from the solidity of its construction but the spirits and seals with which it has been enchanted, ensorcelled, and be-spelled. We've found a round metal snow sled to work very effectively for us. One can paint whatever one wants on the surface, either symbols or pictures or both. Leather shields, as used by the Native Americans are also an interesting means of shield making. Once at a flea market, we acquired a round shield that was made on a round wooden frame covered with canvas that had been painted black. Norse runes had been painted on it in silver, and from its edges dangled fringes of horsehair with Mexican coins tied to it. It was really quite magical. (Hyemeyohsts Storm's book *Seven Arrows* has wonderful examples of Native American shields that can serve as inspiration for the wizard. It is good to note that the ancient elves and the ancient Native Americans were very similar in many ways, often sharing dress styles and spiritual philosophies. Also, you may find interesting the book *American Elves: An Encyclopedia of Little People from the Lore of 380 Ethnic Groups of the Western Hemisphere* by John E. Roth.)

Blue Magic Ceremony

You know the ritual: cleanse and prepare the circle (white magic), secure the circle (black magic), approach it with the right vibrations, attitude (green magic), have your tools ready (orange magic), be prepared to improvise if necessary (purple magic), gather together the right people for the magic (red magic) …

Place the name or sigil, or both, of Enki to the south, Farynder to the West, Zarvan to the North and Tatatyn to the East. If you have reached this magic you should, if you desire them, now have obtained assistants and colleagues. You can assign to them any of the various roles or monologues that follows:

"OH, GREAT SPIRITS OF KNOWLEDGE AND WISDOM, MIGHTY DJINN OF THE SECRET WAYS, REVEAL TO US THE HIDDEN AND ANCIENT MYSTERIES, AWAKEN OUR MINDS AND ILLUMINATE OUR SOULS, FILL US WITH THE POWER TO USE OUR MINDS TO THEIR FULLEST CAPACITY, UNSHACKLE OUR BEINGS SO THAT OUR OWN TRUE GENIUS MAY MANIFEST AND ILLUMINATE THE WORLD."

(Picking up the shield or having a shield bearer carry it in front of you as you progress counterclockwise around the circle say:)

"I ESTABLISH A SANCTUARY WHEREIN FREE SPIRITS MAY COME TO FULFILL THEIR DESTINIES, EXPLORE THEIR SOULS AND THE FURTHEST REACHES OF THEIR MINDS; DEVELOP THEIR BEINGS TO THEIR GREATEST PERFECTION, FREE FROM THE INTERFERENCE OF THE WORLD, THE INTRUSION OF THE UNWANTED AND THE PRYING EYES OF THE ENVIOUS. ALL WHO COME, COME FREELY, ALL WHO STAY DO SO OF THEIR OWN ACCORD, ALL WHO LEAVE FOLLOW THE DICTATES OF THEIR OWN HEARTS AND DESTINY. EVER FREE, EACH ONE FREE, TO COME, TO GO, TO BE, NOW AND FOR ETERNITY. WE ESTABLISH THIS REALM WHEREVER WE GO, IT SURROUNDS US FOREVER, PROTECTS US AS WE GROW, YET IN NO WAY DOES IT LIMIT OUR FREEDOM TO BE, EVER FREE, EVER FREE, EACH AND EVERY ONE.

"SHIELD OF PROTECTION, SHIELD OF OUR TRIBE, PROUD TO BE TOGETHER, NO NEED TO HIDE, SECURE IN THE KNOWLEDGE OUR LIVES HAVE REVEALED, NO NEED TO BOW, NO NEED TO KNEEL, WE STAND TALL IN THE SUNLIGHT, STAND TALL IN THE DARK, OUR VOICES A BEACON TO WHICH OUR KINDRED DO HARK. HEAR US, OH KINDRED, GET BEHIND OUR SHIELD, IF WE STAND TOGETHER WE NEED NEVER YIELD TO BULLIES AND TYRANTS AND "GODS ALMIGHTY", FOR TOGETHER WE STAND AND ESTABLISH OUR RIGHT TO BE FOREVER FREE ... FREE MINDS, FREE SOULS, FREE BODIES, FREE SPIRITS."

(Now, take up the Staff of Power and Wisdom and say, while moving clockwise:)

"I CHANNEL THE CREATIVE POWER OF THE UNIVERSE, INITIATING NEW REALMS OF BEING, INVENTING NEW FORMS OF THOUGHT THAT INCREASE OUR SUCCESS IN LIFE AWAKENING US TO VASTER, MORE POWERFUL AND MORE COMPREHENSIVE WORLDS. I AM FILLED WITH THE POWER TO MANIFEST WHATEVER MY MIND CAN CONCEIVE, MY HEART DESIRE, MY SPIRIT NEED. I SEND VIBRATIONS OUTWARD, AWAKENING KINDRED SPIRITS AND DRAWING THEM TO ME/US. I CREATE A WORLD WHERE GENIUS MANIFESTS DAILY, WHERE LOVE REIGNS, WHERE SUCCESS AND ABUNDANCE ARE ASSURED FOR THOSE WHO STRIVE TO UNLEASH THEIR PERSONAL STYLE AND MAGIC.

"I ENERGIZE THE ENVIRONMENT SO IT SHALL BE CONDUCIVE TO BRILLIANCE, AND INSPIRING TO THOSE WHO ENTER HERE. I ENERGIZE MY PERSONAL AURA SO I WILL BE FOREVER SURROUNDED WITH NEW AND EXCITING POSSIBILITIES, AFFECTING ALL WHO COME NEAR ME WITH A SENSE OF PURPOSE AND POSSIBILITY. I FILL MY WORLD

WITH WONDER. I FILL MY WORLD WITH AWE. I FILL MY WORLD WITH ADVENTURE AND I SEND FORTH THE CALL TO ALL WHOSE SOULS ARE ACHING FOR A NEW AND BETTER LIFE FILLED WITH MYSTERY AND ADVENTURE IN A LAND WHERE LOVE IS RIFE. EVERYWHERE, EVERYWHERE, ALL THE TIME, NOW, FROM WAKING TO SLEEPING, IN DREAMS AND FANTASIES, IN ALL WE DO, IN ALL WE SAY, ON EVERY DAY, IN EVERY WAY, WITH EVERYONE WHO COMES AND GOES, WITH EVERYONE WHO GOES AND COMES, WITH EACH WHO STAYS, THIS VERY DAY, THIS VERY DAY AND EVERY NIGHT THEREAFTER, THE HEARTACHE, THE TEARS, THE STRUGGLES AND DISASTERS SHALL BE REPLACED WITH JOY, AND FUN, AND LAUGHTER. BY MY POWER MANIFEST, BY OUR POWERS JOINED, WE UNLEASH OUR WILL TO NOW FULFILL OUR GENIUS. SO IT IS. SO SHALL IT BE, NOW TO ETERNITY."

(NOW TAKE UP THE LAMP AND SHINING IT AROUND SAY:)

"I ILLUMINATE MY LIFE AND INTELLECT, FILLING EVERY ASPECT OF MY BEING WITH THE RADIANT LIGHT OF INTELLIGENCE AND WISDOM. I BECOME INCREASINGLY CONSCIOUS OF ALL THAT IS AROUND ME, AWARE OF THE MYRIAD FACTS AND INFORMATION FROM THE SMALLEST TO THE LARGEST DETAIL, INTEGRATING THEM INTO A TOTAL AWARENESS OF THE CONNECTIVE TISSUES AND FIBERS OF LIFE. I SHED LIGHT INTO THE DARKEST CORNERS, REVEALING THE MYSTERIES OF LIFE, CREATING CLARITY WHERE THERE WAS UNCERTAINTY, ORDER WHERE THERE WAS CHAOS, AND LETTING THE TRUTH STAND FORTH TO CHALLENGE THE FALSE, AND BY ITS SUBSTANCE REVEAL FALSEHOOD FOR THE PHANTOM IT TRULY IS.

"I OPEN MY MIND TO THE LIGHT OF TRUTH, THE EXCITEMENT OF REVELATION AND THE KNOWLEDGE AND WISDOM OF THE ANCIENTS. I OPEN MY HEART TO THE INSPIRATION AND PURE GENIUS OF THE YOUNG, THE PRIMITIVE, AND THE NATURAL. I AM UPLIFTED BY MY EVERY EXPERIENCE AND EVERY THING I LEARN SERVES TO MAKE MANIFEST MORE CLEARLY THE LAWS AND WAYS OF NATURE AND THE MEANS BY WHICH MAGIC MAY BE SET IN MOTION.

"I ILLUMINATE THE LIVES OF ALL WHO COME IN CONTACT WITH ME, THROUGH INTELLIGENCE, AND HUMOR, KINDNESS AND INSPIRATION, AWAKENING THEM TO THE POSSIBILITIES AND POTENTIAL OF THEIR OWN GENIUS MANIFEST. THEY ACCEPT ME WITHOUT RESISTANCE AND FURTHER MY WORK IN ALL THAT I DO. THEY RENDER ME RESPECT AND I, THROUGH THE INTEGRITY OF MY BEING, AWAKEN THEM TO THE ESSENTIAL DIGNITY OF THEIR OWN SOUL AND SPIRIT.

"I ILLUMINATE THE PATH FOR ALL TO SEE, SO THOSE LOST MIGHT BE FOUND, AND THE WAY UNSEEN CLARIFIED, AND THE MEANS REVEALED, AND THE PURPOSE UNDERSTANDABLE TO THE SIMPLEST OF MINDS, SO THAT ALL WILLS WILL UNITE TOWARD THE FULFILLMENT OF THIS GREAT WORK, THE LIBERATION OF THE SPIRIT, THE MIND, THE SOUL AND THE BODY, SO THAT EACH AND ALL MAY REALIZE THEIR OWN TRUE S'ELF AND DEVELOP THEM TO THEIR FULLEST POTENTIAL. SO IT IS, SO SHALL IT BE, NOW AND FOR ETERNITY."

(Take up the Book of Shadows and open it and display it to all gathered there both physically and spiritually.)

"HERE IS THE BOOK OF SHADOWS, A TRUE JOURNAL OF OUR/MY EXPERIENCES IN THE REALMS OF MAGIC AND BY ITS POWER WE SHALL EXTEND OUR INFLUENCE ACROSS SPACE AND THROUGH TIME, TOUCHING THE LIVES OF THOSE NOT YET BORN ON PLANETS GALAXIES AWAY... TOUCH OUR OWN LIVES IN THE FUTURE SO THAT WE WILL BE INSPIRED BY WHAT WE HAVE LEARNED IN THE PAST. SPEAK ONLY TRUTH HERE, WRITE ONLY LIGHT, SO THAT THOSE THAT COME AFTER MAY SEE CLEARLY THE WAY TO THE SUCCESS WE HAVE ACHIEVED AND THE OBSTACLES WE'VE ENCOUNTERED AND OVERCOME.

"I DO SANCTIFY THIS BOOK SO THAT THE WORDS WRITTEN WITHIN WILL ILLUMINATE THE HEARTS AND MINDS OF THOSE WHO READ THEM, AND FROM THEM OTHERS WILL BE AFFECTED BY THESE IDEAS, EACH BORN OF THE OTHER IN A NEVER ENDING SPIRAL OF EVOLVING INTELLIGENCE, EACH LEARNING FROM THE PREVIOUS AND ADDING TO IT.

"BY THE POWER OF THIS BOOK WE SHARE WITH THE MINDS OF THE FUTURE THE GENIUS OF TODAY AND SPARK WITHIN THEM THE FIRE OF THEIR OWN GENIUS TO LIGHT THE WAY FOR OTHERS STILL TO COME, A TORCH PASSED ON IN ENDLESS PROGRESSION THROUGH THE GENERATIONS TO LIGHT THE WAY TO A BETTER LIFE FOR ALL TO COME.

"TAKE WHAT I OFFER FREELY AND MAKE IT YOUR OWN, TAKE IT TO HEART, TAKE IT ON HOME, CHANGE IT TO SUIT YOU, MAKE IT YOUR OWN, MAKE IT YOUR OWN. OUR MINDS UNITED EXTEND OUR REACH TOWARD ALL WE DESIRE AND ALL THAT WE SEEK. ONE PLUS ONE IN MATH MAKES TWO BUT IN LIFE AND NATURE IT OFTEN MAKES

THREE OR MORE IF YOU SEE. IT'S THE MAGIC OF CREATION AND IT SETS US FREE.

"AND SO WE RECORD IT SO OTHERS MIGHT LEARN AND NOT HAVE TO PLOW EARTH ALREADY TURNED, IN OUR SEARCH FOR WISDOM, AND FULFILLMENT, AND JOY, FOR ECSTATIC REVELATION ON OUR VOYAGE THROUGH TIME AS WE STAND IN THIS PLACE, ALIVE ON A PLANET WHIRLING THOUGH SPACE. SO IT IS, SO SHALL IT BE, FOR NOW AND IN ETERNITY."

(THANK THE spirits. Release the Magic. Open the circle and go forth inspired.)

CHAPTER 3:

YELLOW MAGIC

Yellow Magic is the magic of Harmony and group interaction. While the Red Magic involved the romantic pair, and from that pair the two becomes three, which is the family, thus the coven/vortex, the Yellow Magic extends the coven or group from one to many and promotes harmony not only within the group but also among a number of divergent groups. With the Yellow Magic, one can create group identity and bonding while avoiding competition and conflict with other groups. The Yellow Magic is the magick best suited for developing and promoting world and intergalactic peace.

Life is an intelligence test. Life evolves through the interaction of opposing forces. The key to life is to allow and promote uniqueness and individuality while encouraging harmony and beneficent and tolerant interaction. The Dominance Bureaucracy promotes a society of robots and clones, and structures life so only those at the very top can make any decisions or changes. Everyone is "made in the image and likeness of God" (clones) and yet somehow they are not meant to think for thems'elves, or rule their own lives as "God" does, except in sanctioned ways. Each "man" becomes the King (god) of his home ruling the lives of his family and dominating everyone. This rigid and fiercely stratified social model, however, is constricted by its own prohibitions to action and thought, and inevitably collapses under the weight, pressure and necessity for change and flexibility that life and nature demand. It is for this reason, and the fact that people are as different as they are the same that the Seelie elf principles of individual initiative and independent thought and action are allowed to exist, usually in the form of tolerated eccentrics, musicians, artists, etc., and thus creating a more successful society. Societies that do not tolerate eccentrics are, by their nature, less intelligent, less flexible societies, and less likely to allow the sorts of innovative changes that help a culture endure through time. (see Eccentrics: *A Study of Sanity and Strangeness* by David Weeks and Jamie James. Also see *The Soul's Code: In Search of Character and Calling* by James Hillman.) Elves, when we are tolerated in Dominance cultures, are usually tolerated because of our unique genius. They need us and thus they don't eliminate us.

However, the pressure to conform is immense both for individuals and groups and is constantly used by the "God squad" to keep people in line. They promote conflicts between individuals and groups, and use the constant threat and reality of war among different religious, political and cultural groups to force individuals to seek the protection and security of aligning thems'elves with the "Great One'. It is for this reason among others that the Dominance crowd constantly creates an atmosphere of potential war and why Seelie elves constantly strive to create a peaceful and tolerant acceptance of differences wherein individuality will be nurtured and fostered.

The Dominance Clique promotes conflict in order to unite everyone eventually in one Empire under the Glorious Leader. This is a form of nuclear fission. We Seelie elves promote tolerance among various groups and individuals to promote uniqueness and cultural diversification, which is a form of nuclear fusion. It is only by accepting the right of others to be different that one can preserve hir own uniqueness.

Note: this is in great part is due to the transition from the Age of Pisces to the Age of Aquarius, which also is occurring as the 5th sub-race of the 5th root race, gives way (unwillingly) to the 6th sub-race (check out the Theosophical writings of Blavatsky and the Blue Books of Alice Bailey for more on this). The Piscean age has a theme of good/bad, black versus white, and is represented in the American court system by two sides each arguing an opposing case. The idea is that through the conflict of opposites the truth will come out. (The old idea of the good guy cowboy wearing the white hat and the bad guy wearing the black in old movies and television shows stems from these notions.)

The fourth ray aspect of the seven rays, in the Piscean age has the motto, "Harmony through Conflict", which accords with this theme. However, the 6th sub-race comes into being under the auspices of the Aquarian age, whose theme is "live and let live," and whose fourth ray motto is, "Harmony through Diversity." The 6th sub-race is, by its nature, more accepting of the 5th sub-race, than the 5th sub-race is of the 6th who they often fear, hate, and despise. There is inevitably a conflict between the 5th sub-race folk and the 6th sub-race (elfin and faerie) folk. This conflict is due to the fact that the 5th sub-race doesn't wish to let go of its control of society, and they think they are right about everything, and everyone who disagrees with them is wrong.

However, the 6th sub-race, due to its nature, is not very inclined toward the sort of conflict the 5th sub-race is inculcated toward. The 6th sub-race is more intuitive, more intelligent, and for the most part more appreciative of and capable of humor than the 5th sub-race. The 5th sub-race loves shouting and vitriol as its tools of persuasion. The 6th uses scorn and derision cloaked in humor. The 5th sub-race guffaws at practical jokes, while the 6th loves sly humor.

There is not a strict division between the 5th and 6th sub-races, as the 5th people like to imagine. First, blood and familial ties usually relate them. And, second, there are many who are a bit of both still. Part elf, so to speak, or part faerie and part normal man or woman. So this transition will be affected not by a sudden sweeping change as the 5th sub-race likes to imagine, and tends to fantasize, fearfully, about. They imagine being totally eliminated or, alternatively, wiping out their enemies. The transformation/transition however will actually occur for the most part by a gradual replacement of the types until there will be so many elf, faerie 6th sub-race types about that the ways of the 5th sub-race simply tend to disappear, like clothes gone out of fashion. This process will take hundreds of years and we are just at the very beginnings of it as this book is being written.

The differences in the magics of the 5th and 6th sub-races follow the same divisions. The 5th sub-race imagines magical battles between good and evil magicians. The 6th sub-race tends to do their magic for healing, world peace, and personal fulfillment without having to diminish others by doing so. The 5th magicians order spirits about, dominating them. The 6th ascribe to mutually beneficial bargains and agreements. To the mind of the 5th sub-race magicians, such bargains always turn on you. Magic always costs you for doing it. To the 6th sub-race magicians, magic costs the energy you need to put into it, like weight-training, and magical bargains don't turn bad if you make them with reliable and trust worthy spirits. For the 5th, magic is about power over others. For the 6th, it is about power and success shared.

The Dominance Cliques are typically exclusive. If you belong to one group you can't belong to another. Seelie elf clans are ever open and promote group interchangeability. The more our members belong to other groups, the greater our connections. Our group adhesion is not created by forcing people to make a choice between us or some other group, but simply by natural attraction. Those who are with us are with us because they want to be. When they wish to be elsewhere, they are. It is the joy of being together that unites us, not the fear of being alone.

In the military they have rules against officers fraternizing with enlisted soldiers. This is to preserve the sense of power and authority in the officers, which would be diminished in their eyes if the troops knew them to be human and fallible instead of distant and God-like. The Dominance society creates classes of wealth and privilege and although it seldom fosters fascism overtly, it reinforces continually its satanic underpinnings. This is why racism is so manifestly present in the prison system, and why homosexuality, which is frowned upon by dominating societies, is rampant in prisons. Watch cop shows on TV and notice how the police constantly use the threat of rape and violence in prison to intimidate people into talking. Watch how frequently the "hero" beats (tortures) a person into informing. The Dominance system relies on the terror created by racism and prejudice to keep the "sheep" from straying. What else is a sheep dog for but to remind the sheep of the wolf.

You may also observe that in societies where drugs or alcohol, or whatever, is illegal, there's always a call for more and more police and jails to solve the problem, but the big dealers are seldom caught and the problem is never solved. The rich dominators control the government. The rich dominators control the drugs. They keep them illegal to keep the prices high and they use the drug enforcement agencies to eliminate the competition… the independents who aspire to drug wealth themselves. This is the way of the "God-Satan" Pact. If you would be free of it, you need to avoid the mindless prejudice that keeps it in power. We are not opposed to wealth, far from it. We are opposed to exclusive wealth. To be a Seelie elf is not to gain control over other peoples lives, but to seize control of our own lives, while encouraging others to do the same for their own s'elves.

THE MOTTO OF THE DOMINANCE CLIQUE IS "DIVIDE AND CONQUER". THE SEELIE ELF MOTTO IS, "UNITED WE SHALL OVERCOME."

Peace Pipe

The peace pipe is another form of the wand and we associate it to the element/state of fire/radiance. It is, like the cup/chalice, an instrument of communion; however, the cup is a water/liquid element/state and represents a communion of emotion and feeling, the commingling of those drawn together through natural attraction. While the pipe, being fire/radiance related, symbolizes the communion of people drawn and held together, not by feeling, but by spirit, purpose and will power. The peace pipe represents the determination of diverse and divergent peoples to live and let live despite their differences. Note that because the peace pipe involves smoke it is also associated with the air/gaseous element/state. Some magical tools, as you have surely noticed, evoke complimentary elements.

Also, because the peace pipe involves smoke, it is related to the smudge stick and incense, although neither the smudge nor incense involve the magician's breath, (except if one blows on the smudge stick) as much as the peace pipe. Because of the breath involved, the peace pipe becomes a more intimate magical tool. The magician's breath activates, ensouls, and ensorcels the smoke. And as you may have noticed, as the pipe is passed about each magician touches hir lips to the pipe in a sort of vicarious kissing, and sharing of DNA. In a way, we might say the incense and smudging are like shaking hands with the spirit world. In smoking the pipe, we kiss the spirits.

Creating discord and mistrust, envy and intolerance is a relatively easy matter, although the consequences can be tragic for all concerned. Yet, it is that very tragic state that often compels people to strive toward that more difficult state of peace and harmony, trust and fairness. Peace is a product of tremendously concentrated and focused power; however, the effects of peace are regenerative and lead to increasing abundance and happiness. Conflict, on the other hand, requires little effort at all to get going, yet once happening eventually tends to suck you dry consuming all your time, resources and energy.

What you smoke in the pipe is up to you. Traditionally, it has been a substance that has helped light up/enlighten the minds of those who share it, lifting them to a new level of experience together. Note that Jeremy Narby tells us in *The Cosmic Serpent* that the South American shamans say that tobacco is the grandchild of the spirit world. Thus tobacco is often used as an offering to the spirit world; however, we would advise using natural tobaccos, instead of those treated with various poisons and additives. Note that the smoke of the pipe is often not inhaled so much as blown out. It combines one's breath/prana with the smoke as it is offered to the spirits as previously indicated.

The peace pipe has traditionally been smoked to seal a covenant or treaty in Native American traditions. We elves also use it in this way to seal a covenant between the spirits and us; and in the Red Magic to seal a covenant among the members of our Magic Circle. The same is true of the cigars often used as offerings in Hoodoo and Voudoun, the magician/priest puffs/blows outward through the cigar sending the smoke into the air and the realm of the spirits. (Note: the same is true of liquor used in these ceremonies. Often the magician/priest/Houngan/Mambo takes the liquor into their mouth, but sHe does not swallow, rather sHe sprays the liquor outward onto the various teraphim and idols, or onto the altar where the idols house the spirits. (In this way, liquor is associated with holy water, or spirit water as we elves tend to call it. Note that liquor is often referred to as Spirits or alcoholic spirits. There is a reason for this.)

Rings of Power and Frasority

The magic rings are a symbol of power and frasority (a word we created that combines fraternity and sorority and is more appropriate than either of those words for describing Elven groups). We have assigned them to the element/state of water/liquid since the rings are indicative of unified emotions and experiences. Of course, wedding rings immediately come to mind, but more appropriate to the rings meant here are class rings, the bishop's ring, the cardinal's ring, West Point rings, Masonic rings, etc. Rings that indicate the development of power and authority gained through merit as well as participation in, and association with, a group, lodge, coven, or other frasority.

While we have used the ring as an example, it could be any article that is shared by all the members of the group, such as a talisman or even a tattoo. The object is merely meant to identify, as a black belt does, those who have endured and succeeded in a particular course of study, training, adventure, quest, etc. (*The Fellowship of the Ring*). The British, for example, have school ties and regimental ties (the article of clothing but the idea of connection is obviously implicit). The rings therefore symbolize the integrity of one's group, in contrast to the peace pipe that symbolizes the ability for different groups to intermingle. The ring can also indicate one's ability to preserve hir integrity, dignity and individuality and unique cultural identity within the process of intermingling.

Rings are often also used to symbolize the "higher group", to act as an identification of those who have come together and have united beyond the individual group. Thus again we have the example of *The Fellowship of the Ring*, although in this case their identifying symbol came to be the Leaves of Lorien. Often pin-on buttons are used for this purpose, signifying a particular event where the groups and individuals come together. T-shirts and sweatshirts with the unifying event printed on them are also commonly used. Again, the point is that the shared experience is remembered in order to promote harmony in the future. It is not the object itself that is important but its power to remind us of our commonality and the success that was achieved through unity and combined effort.

The Rings in *The Lord of the Rings* were originally meant to be of this type. Each one was meant to be a ring of power in its own right, but at the same time signifying the united power of those who wore them. Alas, the One Ring was designed as a Master Ring to rule them all and thus betrayed the frasority that the rings represented. In the books, the Fellowship of the Ring was composed of those who sought to destroy the ring. But one could also make a case that the original Frasority of the Ring was composed of the Ring Bearers.

We are not here, however, to ruminate on Tolkien's works, as wonderful as they are, or as much as we love them. And we do love them truly. We are here to indicate that some small token of union that is shared by all the members of a clan, coven, elven vortex and so forth, whether it be a ring, a brooch, or some other symbol, can be a powerful talisman of one's magic. If you have a group or coven, you may consider creating a talisman that denotes your union and the experiences and magic you share. Note that the seven-pointed star, originally used in this era by the Elf Queen's Daughters, of which these elves were a part, as a symbol for the elven people is now commonly called the elf star and faerie star and used by elfin/faerie folk around the world to represent our people.

The Bell

The Bell is an air/gaseous elemental/state tool, designed for several purposes. It can call both humans and spirits to notice a particular magic. It can also be used as a warning to hostile spirits to depart forthwith or suffer the consequences. Bells are often used to announce the approach of the spirit. Their vibrational tones resonate on the spirit planes.

Bells have been used to summon people to church/temple, to school, to gather to deal with fires, invasion, or other disasters. They thus symbolize the call to unity and concerted effort toward the fulfillment of a specific and shared goal.

Since bells are loud and their tone penetrating, they symbolize unity on a far reaching scale, the ability to draw together in need, and/or for purpose, those who otherwise live in widely diverse ways, each pursuing their individual activity until the call for unity comes, and who return to their individual efforts when the need and purpose is fulfilled, or the danger overcome.

Chimes are also included here as a possible alternative, as are gongs, cymbals, etc. All these items resonate, and it is this resonance that is so important in its penetrative ability. Note that monks and priests use resonant tones when chanting, praying and evoking the Spirit. Thus also the magician's voice can become a type of bell or chime, and we suggest when enacting the rituals and ceremonies of this tome that the elves doing so resonate the evocations. A Catholic mass, particularly an old fashioned one said in Latin, is a good example of resonant evocation. Or one could listen to Gregorian Chants, or Tibetan Monks chanting sutras to get an understanding of this technique. For elves it would also work to sing the evocations.

You probably do not wish to make the magic seem silly, unless you are evoking the spirits of humor. A deep respect for the magic is advised, and resonant tones help add to the sense of power, reverence and efficacy to one's magic. On the other hand, neither do you wish to proceed with an overly serious and ponderous/pompous attitude. A reverent attitude united with intent practicality usually work best. A concentration on completing the magic smoothly combined with devoted intention to detail serve the elfin magician well. However, each elf must decide for hir own s'elf the tone/resonance of hir magic.

There is a saying, Do Unto Others As You Would Have Them Do Unto You. Well, in terms of magic, Have the Same Attitude Toward Your Magic That You Want Others To Have Toward You. If you wish respect, treat your magic, and your spirits, respectfully. If you wish people to take you seriously, take your magic seriously. If you wish people to believe in you, believe in your magic. In doing magic, you are creating your own world, your eald, your magical realm, and you are the principle architect of that world. Remember, your magic is the center and source of your universe, just as The Magic is the center and source of all Being.

Coat of Arms/Seal of Radiance

The Coat of Arms is another form of the shield and is related to the earth/solid element/state. It is a symbol, like a flag, of a people, tribe, family, clan, nation, etc. It indicates one's right and power to be individual and unique, and to share that uniqueness while residing side by side with other unique beings. The coat of arms can be put on a flag, banner, shield, gonfalon or other device. We elves sometimes call it the Seal of Radiance. Note the patches worn by students of Hogwarts in the Harry Potter books and movies of the school or their particular house, Ravensclaw, etc., is an example of a Coat of Arms or Seal of Radiance.

If you do not have a personal, or group Coat of Arms, or Trademark, you can create one (as did the ancestors of those who do have a Coat of Arms). Try to incorporate the symbols that are most indicative and descriptive of your s'elf, family, coven, etc. Among the elves, when two families unite through marriage the new family might have a coat of arms that was half one family and half the other. Wood Elves often have trees on theirs. Sea Elves may have water, and/or ships or sea creatures, or the stars they use for navigation. It could contain the totem of each member, or some commingling there of.

It is, of course, not necessary to have a Seal of Radiance. It is not a vital or essential part of the magic; however, it can add much to the sense of community particularly when the seal is attractive and indicative of what the group is about. It is no more necessary to have one than a school needs a mascot and symbol for its sports teams; but it does add to the identity of the school and the Seal of Radiance can add a great deal to your magical family to help it express its unique vision and identity.

For the Yellow magical ceremony, use your personal, or coven/group coat of arms/seal of radiance, drawn in the middle of the double circle. This magic circle is the center of your evolving Eald, the focal point of your magical family and clan.

Yellow Magic Ceremony

Put Enki's name to the south, Avalae to the west, your name or the name of your group/coven, etc. to the north, and Welolynver to the east. You know the ritual: white magic, cleanse; black, secure; green, positive activation with a vision and purpose; orange, supply what you need for the ceremony; purple, be prepared to improvise, don't stand on tradition; red, invite people who will or can harmonize and activate each other; blue, perform it in the most intelligent and elegant fashion possible, remember in science simplicity and elegance take precedence over the crude, complicated and cumbersome. Remember, elven magick is not only an Art but also a Science.

When everyone is within the protection of the circle and the seals set, all your tools are in position, everyone has been assigned their parts to read, and you are ready, begin by intoning:

"WE STAND TOGETHER UPON THE SYMBOL OF OUR UNITY EMPOWERED BY OUR DETERMINATION TO CREATE A BETTER WORLD FOR ALL. WE CREATE HARMONY HERE AND NOW. WE JOIN TOGETHER HERE AND NOW. WE ARE UNITED HERE AND NOW. WE ACT AS ONE, HERE AND NOW, SO THAT THE FUTURE MAY SEE THE LIVING EFFECTS OF OUR HARMONY. WE LAY TOGETHER, UNITED WE STAND, WE RISE UP TOGETHER TO START A NEW LAND WHERE HARMONY REIGNS WITH LOVE AS ITS MATE, MERGING OUR DESTINY AND SEALING OUR FATE, TO OUR FUTURE TOGETHER AND ALL IT WILL BRING, PROSPERITY, ABUNDANCE AND LIFE ON THE WING.

"WE STAND UPON THE SIGN AND SYMBOL OF OUR UNITY. LET ALL WHO SEE IT KNOW THAT WE ARE AS ONE, UNITED IN OUR PURPOSE AND DEVOTED TO ITS FULFILLMENT. LET ALL WHO STAND WITH IT PROSPER AND KNOW ABUNDANCE, ENJOY THE STRENGTH AND POWER OF UNITY, THE PROTECTION OF THE GROUP AND THE SATISFACTION OF SHARING.

"WE GROW WISER IN OUR MINDS, MERGING, SEEING MORE WITH MANY EYES, KNOWING MORE WITH WIDER EXPERIENCE, CREATING MORE WITH MANY HANDS, LOVING MORE WITH MANY HEARTS."

(CHANT TOGETHER)

"TOGETHER OUR MAGIC IS STRONGER BY FAR."

(Now taking the bell, and ringing it, move clockwise saying:)

"Hear me, oh spirits, harken to me, come ye here and gather so that together we will do great things that we cannot attain alone. Listen, mighty spirits, attend to my/our will, and together we shall create abundance to fulfill all our desires.

"Get you gone, interfering spirits, for you shall be trod upon if you stand in our way, for it is our way that we pursue, and our right by destiny to pursue it. Those who block our path have lost their own way and shall suffer the consequences of having done so. Be you gone, this is your warning. We approach and will do none any harm save those who refuse to yield to us the way that is ours, by right and in truth. Get ye gone.

"Hear us, kindred spirits, for you who would join us in the sincerity of your heart with devotion of will, we approach and will receive you with open arms, hasten forth that we might celebrate our reunion, and reunited set about with measured haste the creation of a better world for all.

"Hear us, mighty spirits, know our will, aid us in its fulfillment, join with us in manifesting all that we envision. Protect us from the hatred of the envious. Secure us from the machinations of the wicked, and bring to light our own follies and shortcomings so that in seeing we can overcome them, and thus by our failures learn the way to success and by determined pursuit, find it, by devoted endeavor create it, and through careful construction make it flexible and thus be

ENCOURAGED TO ENDURE. FOR THIS IS OUR WILL, AND IN SO WILLING WE SHALL ENDEAVOR UNTIL ACCOMPLISHMENT, AND UPON ACCOMPLISHMENT STRIVE TO IMPROVE ALL THINGS SO THAT TIME AND INERTIA SHALL NOT BRING THEM DOWN. NO RUST CORRUPT, OR STAGNATION SWALLOW, AND THE FUTURE SHALL SEE AS THE PRESENT OUR RESOLVE UNHINDERED, AND OUR WILL UNDIMINISHED. WE SHALL ACHIEVE. SO IT IS. SO SHALL IT BE, NOW AND FOREVER MORE."

(TAKE UP THE PEACE PIPE. LIGHT IT, TAKE A PUFF AND PASS IT ON SAYING:)

"I SMOKE THE PIPE OF PEACE AND IN SO DOING DEDICATE MYS'ELF TO UNITY AND MUTUAL TOLERANCE AMONG AND BETWEEN OUR PEOPLES. I SWEAR BY MY MIND, MY BODY, MY SPIRIT AND MY SOUL THAT I SHALL HONOR THIS PEACE AS LONG AS YOU DO SO AND SHALL IN NO WAY SEEK TO UNDERMINE IT OR DESTROY IT BY WORD OR DEED, IN PUBLIC OR PRIVATE, IN THE OPEN OR IN SECRET BY ANY MEANS WHATSOEVER, AND I SHALL ENDEAVOR TO FULFILL THE COMPACT OF OUR UNION NOW AND FOREVER MORE."

(ALL OTHERS PRESENT SHOULD EACH REPEAT THIS VOW.)

(AFTER SMOKING THE PIPE SAY:)

"FROM THIS MOMENT FORTH OUR PEOPLES ARE UNITED IN OUR DEDICATION TO LIVE TOGETHER IN PEACE AND HARMONY AND WE SHALL ACT AS ONE BODY WITH TWO HANDS AGAINST THOSE WHO WOULD INTERFERE OR SEEK TO DISRUPT OR DESTROY THIS COVENANT. I DO SO SWEAR. WE ARE ONE, NOW AND FOREVER MORE. WHAT WE HAVE JOINED TOGETHER BEFORE THE SPIRIT LET NONE

SET ASUNDER OR IN SO ENDEAVORING BE SUNDERED THEMS'ELVES. SO IT IS. SO SHALL IT BE. NOW AND FOREVER MORE."

(NOW, TAKING THE RINGS, GIVE ONE TO EACH PERSON PRESENT SAYING:)

"THIS IS THE CIRCLE OF OUR UNITY. IT EXISTS AND LIVES IN EACH AND ALL OF US AND ONCE HAVING COME TOGETHER, NO MATTER HOW FAR THE DISTANCE THAT SEPARATES US IN THE FUTURE, WE SHALL ALWAYS BE TOGETHER IN OUR HEARTS AND MINDS AND THESE RINGS SHALL BRING US INSTANTLY TOGETHER IN SPIRIT.

"I GIVE YOU A RING OF POWER. WEAR IT IN HEALTH. LET IT BRING WEALTH. USE IT WISELY, SO THE CIRCLE OF COMPLETION SHALL BE UNBROKEN."

(REPEAT FOR EACH PERSON.)"

"THOUGH THIS NIGHT WILL PASS, OUR MEMORIES OF THIS CIRCLE SHALL LIVE FOREVER. LET ITS TRUTH CONTINUE IN OUR HEARTS SO THAT THOSE WE TOUCH IN THE FUTURE SHALL FEEL THE EFFECTS OF THIS GATHERING, AS THOUGH THEY HAD BEEN HERE THEMS'ELVES. AND LET US GO FORTH FROM THIS CIRCLE CARRYING IT IN OUR HEARTS SO THAT IT SHALL CONTINUE FOREVER, RESOUNDING IN OUR SOULS THROUGHOUT TIME.

"EMBRACE ME AS I PASS BEYOND THE LINES OF THIS CIRCLE. CARRY WITH YOU ALWAYS THE VISION OF OUR TIME TOGETHER, AND KNOW THAT IN THE FUTURE WE SHALL BE TOGETHER AGAIN IN EVEN GREATER NUMBERS, AND THE MAGIC WE HAVE DONE THIS NIGHT SHALL MULTIPLY THROUGH TIME, INCREASING IN POWER PERPETUALLY IN PERPETUITY."

"KNOW THAT OUR LOVE SHALL REMAIN UNDIMINISHED IN ETERNITY, AND THE BLESSINGS WE HAVE SET IN MOTION THIS NIGHT SHALL INCREASE FOREVER. AND EVERY ACT WE UNDERTAKE IN THE NAME OF THIS CIRCLE SHALL BE A THREAD TYING US TOGETHER, AND ALL THE THREADS TOGETHER SHALL BE A WEB, AND WE SHALL WEAVE THROUGH TIME AND SPACE A TAPESTRY OF HARMONY AND UNION, SUCCESS AND ABUNDANCE, LOVE AND CREATIVITY, AND FROM IT SHALL RISE THE DAWN OF OUR DREAMS GIVING BIRTH TO THE PARADISE OF OUR VISIONS.

"I LOVE YOU. GO IN PEACE. BY THE POWER OF THIS MAGIC I DECLARE IT SHALL BE NOW AND FOREVER MORE, BY THE LIGHT, BY OUR LOVE, NOW AND FOREVER MORE. SO IT IS. SO SHALL IT BE. NOW AND FOREVER MORE.

"LIVE PARADISE NOW! LET ELFIN MANIFEST IN OUR LIVES, AND THROUGH OUR LIVES INTO THE WORLD THE FAERIE MAGIC SPREADS. SO IT IS. SO SHALL IT EVER BE."

CHAPTER 4:

GOLDEN MAGIC

G olden Magic is the magic of evocation, the magic of influencing the spiritual and etheric elements of the netherworld to manifest on the physical plane. Having a baby, for instance, is one form of evocation. It is evoking a spirit/soul into the world. A truly profound and life changing evocation for most individuals.

Evocation is commonly practiced by necromancers, those who communicate with the dead, and sorcerers who delve into the root causes and primordial powers, the source of the world that these elves call The Magic. Modern astrophysicists trying to discover what occurred in the first milliseconds of the "Big Bang" are a form of sorcerers. Those who seek to unlock the genetic code are another batch of sorcerers. Alchemical sorcerers search for the key to atomic structure, the panacea of the ages, and the elixir of life.

Traditionally, evocation is represented by a ceremonial magician summoning up a demon and making a pact with hir to do this or that. And this, in truth, is a form of evocation. But one can also evoke a mood, create an atmosphere, make a particular energy manifest, such as healing energy, peace, abundance or wealth. Thus the golden magic encompasses all the previous magics. Ultimately, the power of evocation enables you to create your own world, your individual universe, first, within your own mind and experience, and then, by the power of evocation, outwardly to impress your Will upon the material plane. With this magic you further your Eald, your personal Elfin/Faerie realm and extend it out into the world, and across the dimensions becoming ever more powerful and influential as you do so. This power reaches across the dimensions and also into the supra-dimensions reaching into the fourth, fifth and higher dimensions of being.

This, of course, entails great responsibility. If you create your own world, you must deal with the consequences, the effects of what you have created. If you create your own world, it's no use blaming God or the Devil if you screw it up. In many ways it's much easier to live in "their" worlds and let "them" take the blame. Although they, in their turn, tell us we have free will and are ultimately responsible anyway. Many folks, particularly the Normal folk, in the face of this, choose to blame the poor, the homeless, those different from them and the eccentric, which is why "their" world has so many cracks in it.

The Dominator societies, composed of the God vs. the Devil forces, tell us we have free will, but that this free will is to be used only to decide to obey, or not. If we obey, we are good, if not, we are part of the demonic forces. Seelie elf magic tells us that we do indeed have free will and we create our lives by all we do. It is not a matter of good vs. bad, but action/magic and the effects thereof, the consequences of that action.

It is exactly these considerations of effects and consequences that confront genetic researchers. If you can create humans by manipulating the genetic code, what type would you create? And what effect on the world do you think it would have? We suggest you create your universe, your Faerie, your Elfin Land, slowly and carefully. Watch it and nurture it, like a child prodigy, so that its genius will unfold and blossom.

Evoking Demons

Evoking demons can be like, yes, exactly like, doing business with the Mafia. As long as it is profitable to them, all is well, but the very first chance they have of screwing you for the money and getting away with it, they will. They can only be trusted in the most limited sense, and since they deal in terror and fear, that is what they understand. You'd have to be pretty tough to deal with the likes of demons, and even then, it's dangerous to do so, for they will betray you at their earliest and most profitable convenience.

This does not mean, however, that they won't pretend to be your very good friend at first, or that they won't, in the beginning, be there for you when you really need them. But this is so you will begin to trust them and so you will become indebted to them. You never, ever wish to be indebted to demons. You don't want to owe them anything. In dealing with demons, you always want it to be under very strict and limited conditions that are clearly and contractually set out. If you deal with demons, whatever they promise you, be sure what you will give them in return is clearly set out, and that you can deliver, and on time. Demons love to angle magicians into being between a rock and a hard place.

However, it is not at all necessary to deal with demons. There are many spirits in the Universe, of many types. Some are advanced helpers of humanity and these and many others are quite trustworthy. Still, care must be taken; even angels are out to fulfill their own duties. Everyone has hir own purposes, goals, and often desires. Mutually beneficial agreements where everyone gets what they want out of things, or most of what they want (compromises are sometimes necessary) is best. And, while they are rare, there are beings who are merely out to help you, to uplift you, with no benefit to thems'elves except the satisfaction of having done so, and the knowledge that the universe will be a better place by virtue of their actions in helping others. Don't count on this, however, nor assume that a spirit presenting itself as selfless truly is so. Always examine your magic carefully. Particularly when it comes to contracts with spirits, which includes human beings for they are spirits, too.

Then, too, not all demons are "evil". Many are simply wild. Think of dealing with a dog or a cat. Or think of a wolf or a bear. Think of a tamed tiger who is, nonetheless, potentially dangerous. Taming demons to assist you can be just like that, a dangerous business and extreme caution is always necessary in dealing with these entities. And remember, even well intentioned spirits can make a foolish mistake. Give your directions carefully. Make them as clear as possible so there is no misunderstanding; and you may wish to caution the spirits against over-energetic behavior. Remember, elemental beings, particularly, can be quite simple, and single-minded creatures, and like children, need a mature guiding hand. Only these are children with tremendous power.

Many folks are horrified by the idea that anyone could delve into magic, and many think evocation and magic in general is a form of Devil worship/Satanism. They also think that they will all die and go to heaven and spend eternity singing their god's praises, which sounds horribly boring to these elves. Would you want to spend eternity in the church choir? Sounds like hell to us. On the other hand, fanatical religious types are such terribly boring people to elves, why should we care what they think?

Therefore, onward to more magic. For we elves love magic. It is truly Divine.

Making Pacts with the Devil

You can trust Satan as much as you can trust a God who will let you be tortured forever for failing to do whatever "He" wants you to do for every second of your life. Or who demands you acknowledge him as your lord and master or suffer the consequences eternally. The Devil is just God with a mask on, being a boogeyman to keep the kiddies in line. The elves are not fooled. We never have been.

The Dominators want clones to do the work for them. Soulless men in grey flannel suits punching in on time like a bunch of robots. Don't give up your soul. Don't sell your soul for success in the world. The Dominator "Gods" do not really want your soul. They have no use for souls. They just don't want you to have one. They just want to repress your soul so they can be constantly reminded of how great they are by seeing how low you'll stoop to kiss their Asses. Did you ever wonder why the ancient witches supposedly kissed the Devil's ass in their ceremonies? It was to teach them how to survive in the world. Always remember if you have to kiss the Devil's ass to get by, at least he has his back to you, and you can pass by unnoticed. And many of us have had to kiss the Devil's ass to survive in the world. But don't give up your soul to do it. As our elf brother, and old and beloved friend Jesus always said, what profits a person if sHe gains the world but gives up hir soul? He, by the way, is appalled at how his teachings have been distorted and coopted by the dominators to enforce obedience in society.

All the tales about people making deals with the Devil to gain great success in the world only to regret it later when their time expired and they had to pay up are cautionary tales meant to awaken people to the fact that in truth the Corporation may downsize at any moment, send the job you were counting on overseas to those who in desperation will sell their souls much cheaper, or that the pension you were counting on was robbed while you weren't looking. To the elves, this doesn't mean one shouldn't work for Corporations, although elves seldom do so, but that they are never to be trusted or counted upon.

Therefore elves are ever using our magic to create Elfin, Faerie, Elfland, a realm where everyone is considered to be an important part of society, and no one, or any group is neglected. This is, of course, an ideal, a fantasy, a dream; but then that is the purpose and power of the magic of Faerie. We make dreams come true. And we do that principally by becoming better individuals, better elves, better magicians, by improving ours'elves in every way, developing all our talents and abilities to their fullest, and every aspect of our being on every plane of manifestation from the material through the mental and feeling planes, into the soulful and spiritual. Doing spells and chants and rituals of magic are all wonderful. But the greatest and most powerful magic we do is in developing our own s'elves, becoming the elves we are destined to be.

Evocation is a Daily Activity

While a magical ceremony communicates your will to the spirits and gives them energy to use to manifest your will, it is in truth your daily actions that are the magical rituals that create/evoke your world and your will. This often means transforming our lives so they will become more and more magical. Part of this is certainly ridding ours'elves of any negative habits that are destructive to ours'elves or others, or in any way counterproductive to our ultimate soulful, magical, and spiritual goals. This usually begins with things we do on the material plane, our actions and habits, but extends in time to our thoughts and feelings. This is a life long activity of ridding ours'elves of feelings of inferiority, thoughts of failure, and anything else that stands in the way of our magical accomplishments. This most often also involves using meditation, or some other discipline, for calming the mind. Ridding the mind of repetitive thoughts, and needless mind chatter and worries, so the mind will become a focused magical tool. Remember two of our most powerful magical tools are a clear and focus mind, allied to serene, yet deep and powerful, feelings.

However, remember this is a lifelong activity. As much as we often wish, particularly when we are young and inexperienced, to have this transformation at all once, it is really about developing life habits. And these seldom occur immediately, but rather after long and continued effort. At the same time, if we are too strict upon ours'elves, our souls, or our bodies, they and the subconscious aspects of our psyche, which are sometimes called our shadow, will surely rebel in time. The idea here is not to dominate yours'elf by having the mind enforce its will on the body, but to become whole through gradual effort that is both good for and rewarding for the whole being. So rid yours'elf of those habits that truly undermine your magic, and allow those things that are mere indulgences but really do no harm if not overindulged.

And as much as possible, live your life with style. Create yours'elf in all that you do. It does no good to march for peace in the world if you come home and badger your wife and children. If you want a world to be a place of love: be loving. If you want sex: be sexy, but most of all remember all magic takes time to manifest. After all, what we are creating is for eternity.

If you wish to be a magician, be a magician everyday in everything you do. Live your magic. By being an elf (or other) in the world, you fill the world with elven magic; by your actions you make elves, and Elfin/Faerie, real. And isn't that what we are here to do? Be who you truly are, who you are meant to be, see your vision of yours'elf and go out and meet it by being that person, as much as you possibly can, here and now, everyday and everyway. That is the true elven magic. And it is by becoming our true s'elves, becoming who we are meant to be, which ultimately means who we truly wish to be, that we find our place in the Universal Order and everything falls into place for us like Magic.

Initiation

When you have achieved the level of the Golden Magic, you are truly ready to initiate others into higher levels of magical development. You, in effect, evoke their "higher", more effective, more magical and fulfilled s'elfhood. You evoke the power of s'elf actualization in them and initiate their "quickening".

When you have attained the Golden Magic, you will affect nearly everyone who comes your way. Whether you make effort to do so or not, your mere presence will create waves of reaction, and you will influence people without any visible intention or effort to do so. The original intention, the intention to develop yours'elf as a spirit and a personality, will now have become an established aspect of your character and will effect changes in the world automatically.

Keep in mind that the people you affect are part of your world. The admonition to do unto others as you would have them do unto you, is not mere homily, but an accurate description of the law of karma. To ignore even the lowliest of those who inhabit your universe is like dressing warmly for a winter storm but leaving your feet bare. It does no good to feed your brain with the greatest education if you starve and poison your body.

The old TV show *The Millionaire* in which a rich man gave a million dollars to a person to see how it affected their life was a form of the Golden Magic. You now have the power to change lives. Use it wisely, for ultimately the life you are changing is your own. Remember you create your world, you own elven realm, your life and your future with everything you do. When you have journeyed this deeply into Elfin, into the Magic, there are no more unintentional acts. Direct intent is no longer, or not always, necessary. Your life is your magical intent made manifest, and everything you do is part of that magic.

Initiate others. Empower them to fulfill their own destiny, to follow their own heart and trust their instincts. Encourage them to think for thems'elves, and to create their own worlds. Give them permission to act on their own initiative, just as we now give you permission to do so. Not that you need our permission; you surely don't, but for those who still feel doubt or uncertainty about their right or ability to evoke the higher magics, to create their own magic, their own eald, we encourage you to do so. It is not that you should give up your doubt, or that you can. Doubts will disappear on their own as you proceed. But you must proceed. You must have the confidence to act, to do your own magic, and create your own bit of Elfin/Faerie, by living your magic. And when we say must, it is not because we demand it of you, but that the Path to Initiation requires it. There is simply no way around it. Just as to be an elf, you must be your own elf. You can't be an elf merely by copying others. You must be your own true s'elf, your own unique elfin magical self. There is no other way.

Treat your others as you treat yours'elf. Encourage them to develop, create and define their own true s'elves and their own elfin magic. Share the magic. Nurture it and watch it grow. For magic is a living being. A being that you evoke into this world and nurture, educate and guide until its influence spreads throughout your life and you and it are one. Be magic and once again, we will live in an age of miracles, and in the magical world of Elfin/Faerie.

Spirit House

The Spirit House is associated with the air/gaseous element/state and is a place, a small home, like a birdhouse, wherein a particular spirit may dwell. This form of magic is very common in the Orient, although it is not exclusive to them. Some people call them faerie houses. The Thai people make very wonderful and elaborate spirit houses.

Faerie houses are, of course, a form of spirit house. Years ago when our children were quite young, we lived upon the banks of a creek that was dry most of the time but would turn into a river sometimes during the rainy season. In fact, so much so that we woke up one morning to find that our house was in the middle of the river and the water just six inches below our floorboards. Before this occurred however we would make faery houses with the children and place them along the river banks among the ferns and other growth to invite our wilder cousins to live near us, and to invite the spirit of Faerie into our lives.

By providing a place for the spirit to live, you are inviting the spirit to spread its power near you and around you. The fact that the house of the spirit, the tabernacle, is small is an indication both that you are providing a private place for the spirit, one in which a human cannot enter, and consequently a sacred place in which the spirit might dwell privately while on the human plane. You are providing it a "place of its own". However, it might be good to realize that the spirit house, like Dr. Who's Tardis is dimensionally bigger on the inside than it appears on the outside. You may enter the spirit house, but not in your mundane body. To enter the realms of spirit one must begin to master the imaginal powers, as every shaman knows. But then nearly any child can do that, and like the old saying about riding a bicycle, one never really forgets how to do it. You just have to trust your imagination. This is also the Way into, through, and about the Faerie realms.

Unlike the temple, which is shared by both the spirit and humanity, the spirit house is a pure manifestation of the spirit on the material plane. In this way, the spirit can manifest completely and without hindrance, and it can also reside in the spirit house, that is have its influence be enduring, and relatively permanent, rather then fleeting and transitory.

Scepter

The Scepter is a variation of the wand, related to the fire/radiance element/state and signifies one's power, authority and regality. It is an implement of leaders, a symbol of aristocracy. However, in this case it is not an arbitrary aristocracy, inherited by birth (although in truth it is passed via the genetic code), but an open aristocracy; one that anyone can earn a place in through their own actions=magic in the course of time. To the elven mind, all elves are royalty, and all beings

80

have within them the seed of the Divine Magic that lives in potentiality in all of creation, but which comes to be realized through our lives, our own magic, and our actions on a daily basis. Thus every elf has the potentiality to express their royal nature, becoming in this way an elf lord or lady, a prince, princess, king or queen among the Elven. And every being has the ability to manifest hir divine nature and become thus a holy person, a saint, sage, or other enlightened and elevated being. In fact, the magic of Elfin/Faerie is such that we may become whatever we wish to be and that is, inevitably, our own true s'elves.

The scepter of the Golden Magic is very much like the wand of Cinderella's Faery God Mother. With it you can transform people's lives, uplifting them, and revealing their true inner beauty and nobility, or lack of it, for all to see. Like a regent, you have the power to instill individuals with knighthood for their efforts and noble deeds. It is traditional that elves and faerie folk have the power to grant wishes. And Tolkien said that Faerie Magic itself is the power to make fantasy a reality. In as much as you can grant other's wishes, help them realize their dreams. This will rebound to you in good karma, but also will return in magic that will help you realize your own dreams. Remember, all we do comes back to us. All we do magically comes back to us multiplied and amplified, and we shape our lives and our future, we create our world by our Being. We are elves because we wish to be elves, and by manifesting as elves we make Elfin real. We are the means through with Faerie manifests into the world.

The scepter can be made of precious metals or stones. It should be beautiful and well decorated and at the same time durable. As we've said previously, the glass wands that are so prevalent at this time are beautiful but often too fragile for this work. It's important that you have a scepter that is well made, and will endure the rigors of use and time. It is symbolic of your magical regency, and you surely wish your realm to endure.

And remember, you deserve this scepter. It is a symbol of your faerie magic and power. Go forth and spread the magic. Realize the dream. Make Elfin real. Be your own elf. Elf Lord, Elf Lady, we bless you. Touch this page; we've instilled a spell of Elfin Blessings here to help you on your way. Te vari elsorin, Eldata Ata. (Be ever blest, Elven One.)

Incense

We might associate incense element/state of earth/solid since, particularly in the magic of evocation, it can be used to provide "substance" for the spirit to manifest in; however, we will instead relegate it to the element/state of water/liquid since its primary value is its ability to evoke a particular mood or atmosphere. Others may consign it to air because it produces smoke. Let each align hir magic as sHe Wishes. What we are endeavoring to convey here is that there is no one right way. There is the way that works for you, which may be different from the way of others, as well as different for you at different times. Elven magic is not only eclectic, but also very adaptable; we alter it as needed, and as our inner guides direct us.

There are books on incense and books of magic that have different scents attributed to this or that spirit but we personally always trust our own intuition and use the scent that seems right in any particular instance. And remember when you are dealing with elfin/faerie spirits, it is best to choose the scent you like, for if you like it then those who are like you, or attracted to you and your magic will surely come. If you are dealing with demons, however, that can be another matter. They can be very picky and persnickety. But once again we advise you, unless you really have to do so, not to deal with demons, they are not to be trusted. And there are plenty of elfin, faerie spirits that you can evoke, who are very trustworthy, although some can be a bit flaky at times. Still, it is also true that many spirits, who are now called demons, are

82

really old demi-gods who have been assigned demonic status by dominator religions. We leave you to judge who is who, and whom you wish to involve yours'elf with magically.

Incense is used, as we said, as a medium for a spirit's manifestation due to its properties of being physical in a visible sense, yet at the same time it is composed of only heat and smoke thus partaking of the etheric insubstantiality of the spirit planes. In this way it brings the two together and serves as a bridge between them. Remember the etheric realm is a physical dimension in the same way that fire and heat are physical. It is subtler, perhaps in some ways we may even say, more refined than more solid matter, but it is definitely physical.

Incense's ability to affect the atmosphere and mood of the magic helps evoke that very necessary and powerful element of feeling and sensory association. It is feeling that empowers the magic. It is the directed ecstatic emotions that charge the magic circle, electrify it with vital energy that enables the spirits to fulfill your will.

When we say directed ecstatic emotion we mean spiritually uplifted, or magically aroused feeling guided by intention. Feelings of out of control anger and rage, while powerful, are not directed emotion. The magician needs to arouse powerful feeling, usually of a higher spiritual state, and guide it, like riding a powerful, spirited horse, to the realization of the magic. Religions strive to create this elevated spiritual feeling, this at-one-ment with the Divine through their magic/religious ceremonies. Shamans strive for this ecstatic state of bliss through chanting, drumming and dancing. We elves seek this elevated, ecstatic feeling of being attuned to, and linked with Elfin/Faerie and The Magic, the source of all things, in this same way. And among these feelings, we include the sense of union and affection that exists among our kindred who enact the magic ritual with us. The sort of esprit de corps that is often found in spiritual groups, a camaraderie of spirit that empowers all those involved, is also a potent energy for empowering the magic. For elves together, nearly all things are possible.

The incense helps enable us to do this as well as creating an experiential clue that may be aroused when that incense is encountered again in the future. This is similar to when couples remember their "song" when they hear it in passing, and it arouses memories of their romance when they were first together. If the ceremony, the magic, is powerful enough then every time you smell that scent, you will be reminded of that magic, and it will resonant further into your consciousness and from there into the world. And this is our goal, to create resonant magic that will ripple outwardly into the world, massaging it with the shimmering magic of Elfin.

The Contract

The contract, covenant, compact is an agreement between beings that is usually written on spirit paper and is associated with the element/state of earth/solid. It defines your will to the spirits and tells what you will do to pay, feed or nurture the spirit in exchange for this service. Traditionally, virgin parchment is used, although a new sheet of unlined paper will suffice. The contract is most often sealed, not with a signature (although that is not excluded) but with a drop of one's vital bodily fluid such as blood, semen, or saliva.

A formal contract is not always necessary, although in dealing with demons it is advised, and in such instances it should be worded carefully, for demons are experts at getting off on technicalities, which is why so many of them go into law as a profession, or study the law when incarcerated. Whereas, angels in general, and the Seelie elf and faerie folk in particular, regard the spirit of the law or contract as more important than technicalities, and a general understanding works well with such beings. When it comes to the elementals, careful wording can also be important, not so much because they, like the demons,

84

are ever seeking a way to get their own way and screw you in the process, but because elementals can be very simple focused beings, rather like children in that way, and need clear guidance and instruction. Needless to say, whether you are dealing with angels, demons, elementals, our faerie kin or other spirits, keeping your side of the agreement is vital.

The contract can also be an agreement between the adept and the aspirant at any particular level, defining what the aspirant must accomplish to achieve the next level of initiation. In this way, it is not greatly different than going to a guidance counselor, or a faculty advisor, or one's thesis or doctoral advisor, and making out a plan of coursework and following through to achieve one's stated goals. In helping others on the path of magic, we first find out what their true will is, and then advise them, as best we may, on how they may proceed to attain that will and what knowledge or skills they need to acquire to do so. These elves are not so formal as to require a contract with our others, but sometimes an outline of what they may wish to pursue can be of great value.

For our own part, on the other hand, we sometimes make lists of the things we wish to achieve with our magic, and one may call this a contract with the spirits, although it is also even more so a contract with our own s'elves. And you may say that when we use spirit paper, inscribing a spirit's glyph upon it to summon that spirit for a particular purpose, and then speaking to it, touching it, putting essential oil upon it, or saying spells and enchantments to it, we are creating and fulfilling a contract between us and the spirit. The details are not written down. It is rather, in a sense, an old-fashioned handshake deal, but it is a contract, a covenant between us.

A Ceremony of Golden Magic

You know the ritual: Purification, Protection, Positive Attitude, Resources, Flexibility, Right Helpers, Right Time, and following the Wiccan Rede: "And that it harm none, do what thou wilt". This, by the way, is a very 6th sub-race Aquarian Age idea and thus very much in keeping with the Elven Way and is part of the reason why elves and witches usually get along so well together. The 5th sub-race motto would be: "Do what you are told to do, or suffer the consequences." Check out the old movie from 1971 of *Simon: King of the Witches* starring Andrew Prine for a scene in which he attends a witches' ritual and the High Priestess tells the witches to kneel and he keeps urging them to "stand up". Here you see a clear distinction between the movement of the 5th and 6th sub-races.

Make your magic circle with Enki's name inscribed between the inner and outer circles to the south, Avalae to the west, Zarvan to the north, and Enanadre to the east. Within the circle have the symbol of your group/coven/vortex. Alternatively, the seven-pointed star can be used for all elven or faerie magical ceremonies.

The Magic Triangle

The Magic Triangle is positioned outside the double circle and is the magical realm wherein the spirit will manifest. Usually, the sigil of the spirit with whom you wish to communicate is drawn within the triangle, or a sheet of spirit paper, or a lamen with the spirit's sigil/glyph/signature is put inside the triangle. Place the incense there as well.

Since this is a ritual of initiation, place the triangle with the point coming toward but not beyond the inner circle. This differs from most evocation where the triangle is placed at a short distance from the circle. The aspirant should begin by standing within the triangle. Here you are not summoning a spirit, elemental, daemon or other being to service but calling forth the inner spirit, the higher nature of the magician who is to be initiated. Initiation is meant to awaken the aspirant's higher nature, hir elfin faerie nature, increase hir powers, and most particularly hir confidence, so sHe will transcend the need to be directed by others and initiate hir own magic.

(Light the incense and then retreat into the circle, seal it, then say:)

"WELCOME, SPIRIT, TELL US YOUR NAME AND STATE YOUR BUSINESS HERE WITH US."

The aspirant then gives hir name and declares hir desire to rise to a particular level of attainment,

"HAVE YOU FULFILLED THE REQUIREMENTS OF THE LEVEL OF _____? "

(Note that among elves this is seldom a title as it is in some magical traditions. We don't tend to have Neophyte, 1° degree 10□, as is the case in Crowley's Lodge. Rather the individual has personal magical goals they have set for thems'elves and upon completion or accomplishment of these sHe is ready to advance to a new quest. Although there is certainly nothing that says such an elfin lodge couldn't be created. However, instead of Neophyte and Zelator, we would probably have various titles of nobility such as Baron, Earl, etc.)

Aspirant: "YES, I HAVE FULFILLED THE CONTRACT/QUEST COMPLETELY AND AS SPECIFIED."

"THEN, IF THIS BE SO THERE ARE NONE WHO CAN GAINSAY YOU, NOR PREVENT YOU FROM ENTERING THIS CIRCLE AS _____."

The aspirant enters the circle, saying:

"THEN I DECLARE THAT I AM _____ AND AM ENTITLED TO ALL RIGHTS AND PRIVILEGES THAT INHERE THEREIN. I DECLARE MY POWER AND INTENTION TO ACT AS A _____ AND WILL PROVE BY MY EVERY ACTION THAT THIS IS SO."

(Picking up the scepter, you say:)

"BY MY POWER AS THE MASTER OF THE TEMPLE/VORTEX OF _____, I ACKNOWLEDGE YOUR RIGHT TO BE CALLED _____ AND PROCLAIM THAT ALL YOUR BROTHERS AND SISTERS DO LIKEWISE. WELCOME TO OUR CIRCLE _____ AND TELL US WHAT YOU WILL TO DO WITH THE POWER OF _____."

(The aspirant steps from the triangle into the circle and says:)

"I PROCLAIM TO ALL PRESENT, TO ALL SPIRITS WHO LISTEN IN, AND ALL WHO MAY BE INTERESTED THAT I WILL _____ AS SET FORTH IN A NEW CONTRACT WITH THE SPIRITS SO THAT UPON FULFILLMENT OF THESE ENDEAVORS/QUESTS I WILL ASCEND TO THE LEVEL OF _____.

"THEN SO BE IT. MAKE YOUR MARK UPON THIS CONTRACT AND SET ABOUT ITS FULFILLMENT WITH OUR BLESSING AND OUR PLEDGE TO AID YOU IN WHATSOEVER WAY IS POSSIBLE FOR US AND MOST BENEFICIAL TO YOU."

Aspirant: "I THANK YOU FOR YOUR GUIDANCE AND ASSISTANCE AND PLEDGE TO USE THE POWERS I ATTAIN

WITH INTEGRITY AND WITH AS MUCH WISDOM AS I CAN MUSTER."

Master of the Ceremony: "IT IS NOT WE ALONE WHO SHALL AIDE YOU BUT THE VERY SPIRITS THEMSELVES AND IN PARTICULAR THE SPIRIT _____, WHO IS YOUR SPECIAL GUARDIAN AND PROTECTOR ON THE LEVEL OF _____. AND TO PROVIDE A PLACE FOR THIS SPIRIT SO THAT IT WILL MANIFEST IN YOUR LIFE AND ASSIST YOU IN ALL YOUR EFFORTS TOWARD THE FULFILLMENT OF YOUR TRUE WILL, WE GIVE YOU THIS SPIRIT HOUSE."

Asp. "I THANK YOU WITH ALL MY HEART AND I SHALL NOW, WITH YOUR ASSISTANCE, SUMMON THE SPIRIT _____ AND PRESENT TO (THE NAME OF THE SPIRIT) THIS TEMPLE IN THE MATERIAL WORLD."

(The aspirant places the spirit house within the triangle and places the lamen or spirit paper that bears the spirit's sigil upon it within the house.)

Asp: "HEAR ME, MIGHTY _____, FOR I DO CALL TO YOU AND INVITE YOU TO APPEAR HERE FOR I DO KNOW YOU TO BE MY FRIEND AND MENTOR, MY GUARDIAN AND PROTECTOR ON THE PLANES OF THE ASTRAL AND NETHER WORLDS, FOR WE HAVE BUILT YOU A HOME, HOWEVER SIMPLE AND HUMBLE, SO THAT YOU MAY EASILY APPEAR IN THIS WORLD AND CARRY OUT OUR WILL. APPEAR, MIGHTY _____, SHOW US A SIGN, FILL THIS HOUSE WITH YOUR SPIRIT AND ACCEPT MY APPRECIATION FOR ALL YOUR AID AND ASSISTANCE.

"SO IT HAS BEEN DONE, SO IT IS, SO SHALL IT BE FOR NOW AND EVERMORE.

"LET US COME TOGETHER, SISTER AND BROTHERS, FOR UNITED OUR INDIVIDUAL POWERS ARE INCREASED MULTIFOLD."

M.C. (Master of Ceremonies): "TOGETHER WE CAN ACCOMPLISH ALL THINGS."

Asp.: "THROUGH YOUR HELP I AM UPLIFTED."

M.C.: "BY YOUR ASSISTANCE I AM SET FREE TO DO GREATER THINGS."

Asp.: "BY THE AIDE OF THE SPIRITS OUR POWERS BECOME UNLIMITED."

M.C. "AND TOGETHER WE CAN ACCOMPLISH ALL THAT WE WILL."

Asp.: "TOGETHER."

M.C.: "TOGETHER."

Asp,: "TOGETHER."

M.C.: "TO GATHER TOGETHER OUR POWERS UNITED, OUR WILLS ALLIED, OUR HEARTS IGNITED, OUR MINDS AS ONE,

OUR BODIES MERGED AND FROM OUR BRIGHT UNION THE MAGIC DOES SURGE."

(Master of Ceremonies takes up the scepter and holds it outward toward the others saying:)

"I RULE MY LIFE."

(Each joining, takes a grip on the scepter and says:)

"I RULE MY LIFE."

M.C., "I AM THE MASTER OF MY DESIRES AND FROM THIS MASTERY COMES THE POWER TO CHANGE THE WORLD."

All others, "I AM THE MASTER OF MY DESIRES AND FROM THIS MASTERY COMES THE POWER TO CHANGE THE WORLD."

(All chanting:) "IN ALL I DO AND ALL I SAY, I CREATE MY WORLD EVERY DAY."

(If you do this chant long enough there should be a tremendous feeling of power running among the participants. When this energy is raised, direct this emotional power into the magic by consciously channeling your emotive power. --- Emote ---- Howl like the wind. Roar like the sea. Let the entire magic power stream out of you and into the spirit house. Feel the power and release it in the direction you will. Like an arrow being released from a bow, it will go to the target with all the force and accuracy you have put behind it.)

"WE SEND THIS MAGIC TO ACHIEVE OUR WILL. IT WILL NOT CEASE TILL OUR WILL'S FULFILLED. IT WILL NOT

YIELD, NOR HESITATE. IT WILL NOT WAVER, NOR PROCRASTINATE, BUT WILL ACHIEVE ALL WE DESIRE, BY THE LIGHT OF DAY AND MOONLIT FIRE. AND WHEN COMPLETED SHALL RETURN TO BE REVIVED AND BORN AGAIN AND THUS RENEWED AND FILLED WITH LIFE, AND CUT THROUGH OBSTACLES LIKE A KNIFE, AND WITH CERTAIN HAND BRING END TO STRIFE. AND ALL SHALL BE AS WE'VE DESIGNED. FOR NOW, FOREVER, THROUGHOUT TIME.

"SO IT HAS BEEN DONE. SO IT IS. SO IT SHALL BE NOW AND FOREVER MORE." 3X.

(Now proceed with the closing of the ceremony. Open the circle and reenter the mundane world. The aspirant should take the spirit house home with hir and put it in some special place. The Master of Ceremonies keeps the new contract(s) and saves it/them until the aspirant has fulfilled its conditions, and is ready for the next initiation. Be especially aware for the next week or so. If your magic has been successful the spirit world will send you a sign or signs to let you know that it has heard you. We cannot say exactly what the sign will be. That depends on the magic you have done and the spirit involved. But we can tell you it should be clear and obvious to you. If you are uncertain about whether it is a sign or not, it's not a sign. Although it is possible an event may occur that is so out of the ordinary that it is clearly a sign, but you may be uncertain what the sign means at first.
When the sign comes, it will be clear to you and you will not doubt or question that it is a sign. However, if you are uncertain of its meaning, it is good to examine it, as one would a dream, to perceive its message to you. If you don't understand yours'elf, you may wish to seek the assistance of the others in your group, and you will surely get an idea of its meaning. The use of Tarot, I Ching [see our Elven Book of Changes: a Magical Interpretation of the I Ching], or other oracles with which you resonate can also be helpful in understanding the sign. You may also wish to check out Jeremy Taylor's books on Dreams and dream interpretation. We studied with him for over a year and he is a true Master of Dream Interpretation.)

CHAPTER 5:

SILVER MAGIC

S ilver Magic is the magic of Invocation, the uniting of the mundane s'elf with the higher spiritual nature, the enlightenment of the individual and hir quantum leap from initiate to initiator. In the Silver Magic the adept transforms from the one who initiates projects to the one who initiates others who initiate projects.

The Silver Magic is the magick of the master magician. This magus seldom reveals hir position to anyone and can often be found playing the part of the novice among other novices. (Hermann Hesse's novel *Journey to the East* shows an example of this.) SHe is always equal to everyone, and yet hir presence creates transformation in all whom sHe encounters. The master mage creates hir own magic.

While most individuals would recognize the Golden level magician as a person of authority and power, only the rarest of individuals are able to recognize the Silver level magician for the master that sHe truly is, for most often sHe appears quite simple and plain to the common eye. All hir power stems from the uniqueness of hir own nature. SHe tends to go unseen and unrecognized unless sHe speaks Words of Power and then people cannot help but pay attention to hir.

To attain the Silver Magic one must be able to trust without exception, and to be true to, even unto death, hir own feelings. There is no magical force more powerful than one's pure feelings; and discovering what your true feelings are, and learning to tune into them is the most significant of magical events. It is through our feelings that we interface with the magical world, particularly the realms of Faerie. Faerie/Elfin calls to us through our feelings. It is our Sense of Faerie that guides us to that magical realm.

The world is filled with philosophies, theories, notions, beliefs and restrictions, but few, if any, have anything to do with your true inner feelings, and the true direction, course and destiny of your life. And many, if not most of them, run counter to our true and natural propensities. To sort out what is right from wrong, what is true and false, what is right and true for us in particular, demands the development of our pure, which is to say non-emotional, feeling. We use emotional to signify feelings that are prompted by thoughts and ideas. Pure feeling is not mediated by thought but arises spontaneously from within the elf, and then arouses thought in the form of intuition.

Before you initiate others, you must first initiate yours'elf; that is, allow your true s'elf and feelings free reign. Where would most governments and religions be if we trusted ours'elves more than we trusted them? Right where most of them belong... right down the toilet!

Unfortunately, getting to one's true feelings is no small or easy task and sorting out what are true feelings from the neurotic complexes that many people have been enculturated to believe to be their s'elves is not easy, and in fact, is truly the work of lifetimes. But every effort we put toward this goal brings tremendous results and our power increases exponentially.

By uniting with our true feelings we bring our fate in harmony with our destiny. We unite our current lifetime with the store of experiences from all our lifetimes, and by becoming more natural, we become more in tune with nature, and thus, more powerful. We move with the cycles of Nature and its power supplements our own.

And as we become ever more attuned with our own nature, thus are not in any way deluded or deceiving ours'elves, so do we become progressively clear sighted concerning others, and it becomes increasingly difficult for anyone to deceive us.

This process, which begins with our first step into the practice of magic, culminates at the Silver Magic when we have merged completely with our true inner s'elves. Once we have done so, we will be both more impressive as beings, and more open to being truly impressed by others. Our relations with others will be direct, sincere and intrinsic. We will gain the ability to absorb the essence of others, to understand them completely without losing our own individuality. (This is what is truly meant in magic tales when one comes to know another's true name and thus gains power over them.) And in thus understanding others, we gain compassion for them for we will also gain an understanding of why they are as they are, as well as being able to intuit the subtle means for helping and influencing them toward improving their lives. At the same time, this openness and naturalness, enables us to absorb the intelligence of others, to learn without resistance, to osmos (osmosis) the essence of any particular subject.

To have attained the Silver Magic is to have freed our personal genius, and more than that, to use that genius to awakening other geniuses. Note the word genius is associated with the word Genie, or Djinn; however, one's personal genius is often called hir daemon. Also, all these are associated with, however somewhat different from, one's Ally in sorcery, and one's Holy Guardian Angel in ceremonial magic.

When we are attuned to our feelings, we become free of doubt and act without hesitation. Our thoughts become clearer, simpler, and more direct. Absent is the confusion of warring philosophies and the battle between enculturation and our inner desires; the war was won by our true feelings that made peace with our minds. Our minds open until they can encompass all that we experience. Our personal certainty and confidence inspires confidence in others, and we affect them without even trying. In fact, trying and effort obstruct the flow of energy, and it is the fact that our influence is effortless that is so astounding to others.

Know your own feelings. Be your true s'elf and you will be in harmony with the all of Nature, and the power of the Universe will support your every action. The Divine inheritance that lives in all beings shall have awakened in you and you will spread the spores and seeds of awakened Divinity wherever you go, whomever you touch, in every word, action and deed. Elfin light will radiate from your being, and everyone who sees you will be blessed to have done so.

However remember, your true feelings are not necessarily your emotions and passions, but live within you in a much deeper realm in the calm sea of your inner being where your true power abides. This is the inner sacred pool of healing and Elven Magic.

Sacred Sacrament

While we entitled this section: Sacred Sacrament, in fact, this is but one means of reaching the goal, which is uniting the inner s'elf with its Divine potential. The sacred sacrament is allied with the fire/radiant element/state since its purpose is the enlightening of the individual. Magical herbs are easily called to mind here and have been in use since prehistory to enlighten the aspirant. However, herbs are but one means and others have included meditation, fasting, endurance of pain, and repetitious/trance music.

Please note that we do not recommend that you use "drugs" for enlightenment; neither do we recommend meditating, fasting, drumming, inflicting pain on yours'elf, nor flirting with near death experience. We simply would be remiss, however, if we did not point out that all these methods and more have been used for eons for awakening the aspirant to greater reality. This is particularly true in the case of herbs/drugs. It should be noted that there are few substances truly suited for this purpose, and there are a great many substances that would seem to achieve the goal but really do not. (It should also be noted that we elves are much more inclined toward pleasurable means of creating and experiencing the ecstatic/enlightened

96

state than painful and/or dangerous ones.) One simple test is addiction. If the "drug" causes addiction, it is not truly enlightening, for enlightenment sets you free. It expands your consciousness. It doesn't restrict it. Nor does it mimic psychosis.

The Satanic/God/Dominance Cabal loves to have people enslaved to addictive drugs, but the true herbs of enlightenment do not enslave you. They set your free. They are instruments of liberation. Some herbs that have been used in this capacity are peyote, psilocybin, cannabis, DMT and LSD. Again, note we do not recommend their use, as it can be extremely dangerous to alter one's consciousness in a robotic society. You are taking your mind in your hands. We merely note that magicians, pioneers and explorers have done so for ages and will continue to do so, and as is the case with all exploration, some will get lost, some fall prey to accidents, some will be destroyed by hostile natives, and yet still we explore. (You may wish to investigate the works of Terence McKenna, Alexander Shulgin, and *DMT: The Spirit Molecule* by Dr. Rick Strassman, as well as Daniel Pinchbeck's *Breaking Open the Head*.)

While we elves are not inclined toward artificial trials of strength and endurance as methods of initiation, there is no question that Nature often confronts us with such tests of courage and persistence. And weight training and other athletic pursues which strengthen us, and we include various martial arts in particular, are often used by the elves to improve our bodies and our sense of well being and confidence. And surely there are numerous elfin who test thems'elves through extreme sports. But we don't usually have such tests set by others. The Way of the Elves is ever one that is guided by the individual and their own inner directives. As their guides and mentors, we help them decide, find and discover what their own goals, visions, and dreams are, and what they feel will help them achieve their will and come closer to their own inner sense of and connection to Elfin/Faerie, as well as, increasing their power as individuals and magicians/magic wielders. Everyone must find hir own way into Elfin, for the threshold always exists within the individual, thus it will ever be a unique and individual journey.

In Catholic, and many other Christian faiths, wine, or sometimes grape juice, is blessed and instilled with the spirit of Jesus to make it a sacred sacrament. The same is done with the bread that is mystically transubstantiated into the Body of Christ. The Catholic priests also bless water to make it Holy Water. We elves can do the same thing, without the need of a priest, for any elf who feels attuned to Faerie has the power to perform this magic. We make the sign of the Elven Star that the Faeries call the Faery Star (we don't mind), over water, or wine, or whatever we chose to use as the substance for the sacrament. These elves often inscribe the seven-pointed Elf Star in an inverted fashion that denotes the downward movement from Elfin/Faerie into the material/mundane world. The upright Elf Star indicates a movement of aspiration from the mundane world toward Elfin/Faerie. Naturally, the elfin magus needs to do this with confidence, with the certainly that sHe is instilling the water, wine, or whatever chosen item, with Faerie magic, and that whomever consumes it will be filled, saturated with Elfin magic. This, you will notice, accords with the old faerie tales and lore that says that anyone who consumes food or drink in Elfin/Faerie will have to remain there for a time. Who would want to leave?

Oils of Anointing

The Oils of Anointing are associated with the water/liquid element/state and although oil and water do not mix the water elemental among the elves is really understood as liquid. It is related to the soul, the feelings, and to be anointed with the sacred oil symbolizes the initiation of the individual into a new, deeper and more comprehensive realm of experience.

While you could use perfume for this purpose, or olive oil, or even water, as the Catholic Church does, we recommend that you use natural perfume oils that can be found in most natural food stores. You can, as we do with spirit water, and the sacred sacrament, inscribe the seven-pointed Elf Star over the oil while keeping in mind your vision, visualizing the power you wish the oil to transmit, and instilling the oil with your intent by the power of your will. You may say a spell while doing so, such as:

UNTO YOU THIS POWER NOW

YOUR BODY I INSTILL

RIPPLING CROSS YOUR SKIN

MY WILL IT DOES FULFILL

DEEP WITHIN YOUR BEING

THE ESSENCE DEEP DOES MERGE

AWAKENED BY MY VISION

ENCHANTMENTS NOW DOTH SURGE

AND EACH ANOINTED WITH ITS TOUCH

IS MOVED TO MAGIC TRUE

AND THROUGH HIR LIFE

DOES FAERIE SHINE

AND MAKE HIR MAGIC TRUE.

Oil, besides being a perfume base, is the source of much of what is created in the modern world. In its simplest form, it has been used for ages as a means of lubrication, and thus it has the added symbolism of easing one's way into a new and vaster reality, literally making life easier for you, or easing your way. For such is the reality of becoming in tune with your true feelings and nature, everything becomes easier because you are doing what comes naturally. You are going with the flow of Nature and in that way adding its power to your own. When you go with the flow of your own being, that is to say when you are fully behind your magic, not in conflict with yours'elf, your magic comes naturally and its power increases exponentially.

And oil has also been used in lamps, thus the Oil of Anointing helps awaken the light within us, although the Oil is not the fire. It is not the light, but the medium that burns. It helps fire endure and thus the Oils of Anointing indicate our own ability to endure the tests and trials that accompany the guest of the Golden Stairs. (While it is somewhat slow reading as a novel in our opinion, you may none-the-less, find Arthur Edward Waite's book *The Quest of the Golden Stairs: A Mystery of Kinghood in Faerie* worth reading. There is much in it that is worthy.)

Elven Book of Spells

The Book of Spells is related to the element/state of air/gas and while similar to the Book of Shadows, differs in that the latter is a book of one's experiences in magic, a journal or diary of your magical life, the book of spells is more of a recipe book, a collection of the various formulas you have encountered and tried for achieving various magical effects.

While the short anecdotes we have written in these books about our personal experiences in magic would be appropriate for a book of shadows, the color magic ceremonies would be best used in a book of spells. However, while a book of spells on the earlier color magics might include those in this or other books, in the silver magic it is important that your book of spells be filled with your own magic, your personal magic that originates from your soul, your personal genius. What you'd probably wish to put in your Elven Book of Spells would be the ways you modified the ceremonies and the results of your ceremonial magick.

The word Spell means both spelling, that is writing out and defining your magic and also spell, as a period of time, reminding us that magic manifests through time, and that it is most powerful for a certain period of time but will not last if not reinforced. Magic, like your body, must be feed regularly. Just as your car needs oil, water, gas and regular maintenance to keep going, so does your magic. Like a loud sound that spreads out into the distance it eventually begins to fade, merging in a sense with its surroundings.

Just a reminder, we are using the term time here as it is commonly used, which is to say as a process in which one moment follows another. In fact, it is always Now. And this is part of what makes magic possible. All that ever was still exists in an altered form in the Eternal Now, and all that will be lives in potential, as yet untransformed, in the Now. When we talk about time we are really talking about change/transformation, sequential development, and movement through Space, or Space/Time. All that exists, all that is, is Now. However, it is spread out through the Universe in overlapping and interconnecting Dimensions. Everything possible is Now, although not everything can be now in the same place/dimension. And some are now in potential, and some are now in realization/manifestation/actuality.

When people say such things as: there can't be good with out evil, and so on, this is technically true as an idea. But the place of good is in manifestation, and the place of evil is in non-realized potential. However, it might be more accurate to talk of harmony and disharmony. Harmony does not need disharmony, except as a concept, to exist. In fact, disharmony precludes harmony, and harmony transforms disharmony. In finding our place in the Universe, in becoming our own unique elfin star, we become part of the great song that is the symphony of Creation, the enchantment/spell cast upon potentiality by our own desire to become ours'elves.

Make your book of spells truly your own and share it with those of us still struggling to bring forth our own magic. Just as painters, and writers, and other artists copy those they like until they find their own style, so do magicians follow in the footsteps of the great ones who have gone before us until we find, create, and sometimes stumble upon our own way. These elves ever hope that the Way we stumble upon will lead us ever deeper into the Radiant Realm we love to call Elfin.

Crown

The crown is related to the earth/solid elemental/state, and is quite obviously the symbol of royalty. To be crowned is to ascend to the realm of the Divine on earth, an event that bears with it both power and privileges, as well as tremendous responsibility. When a King or Queen speaks, they do not say I, but We, because they speak for their entire people. Their lives are no longer their own but are lived for the sake and benefit of their people. To put on the crown is to assume responsibility for one's group. To be an Elven King or Queen is to live one's life for one's people. All one does, all one has, is offered in service of one's elves and others. It is not a position of authority where one tells everyone else what to do and they automatically obey. At least this is not the case with elves. It is rather a position where many come to the king or queen who suggests and hints those things that might be done to make their lives better. Those who come do so of their own accord, and follow the advice of the king or queen, not because they have to do so, but because they recognize the king/queen's wisdom and that following the king/queen's advice will lead them to success.

For the Silver Magic the crown is only worn in the privacy of the magic circle. Out in the world the magus of the Silver

Magic is outwardly indistinguishable from an ordinary person, except, of course, for the exceptions to this rule (there are always exceptions). In the outer world the crown is an invisible one. It is a crown that is only discernable by one's spirit and personality. It is reveled in one's nobility of character. Anyone can attain a crown for thems'elves and pretend to be noble, but true royalty is revealed by one's actions and behavior, and in no other way.

Stories often tell us that the Elven Realms are ruled by Kings and Queens, but this is not so, at least for the Seelie Elves. There is no King of the Elves. However, there are kings and queens among the elven. These individuals dedicate their lives to helping their others. To say that one is a king or a queen among the elven is to say that one aspires to be so great that all they do and all they own is used in service of their people. The Seelie Elves consider it rude for someone to announce on hir own that sHe is a elven king or queen; but if one does so we accept that as a proclamation of intent. This individual is, in effect, saying bring all your troubles to me. When you have need come to me and I will do my best to help you. I will further you in every way I can. Shelter you if needed. Hint to you the way. And pat you encouragingly on the back as you venture forth again.

Being a king or queen among the elves is not a matter of genetics. One is not a queen because hir father was king. Nor is it a matter of being voted as king. One must earn their kingship through their actions. Although, if enough individuals spontaneously consider someone their queen than the individual may, even should, unless otherwise directed by their heart, assume that regency. And every elfin magician is the king or queen of hir own magic circle. As far as the Seelie Elves are concerned, every elf is potentially an elven king or queen. So in the midst of your magic circle wear your crown, if you will, but know in doing so you are proclaiming that you are putting yours'elf forward as the one to come to when any of your kin, elementals, or associative spirits need help and guidance.

Silver Magic Ceremony

You know the Ritual: Purification, Protection, Positive Attitude, Resources, Flexibility, Right Helpers, and Propitious Time.

Make a double circle with the triangle inside the circle. (This is unusual, and is an exception made for this ceremony as you are invoking your own higher spirit. Usually, the triangle is outside and a bit removed from the circle.) Have your elven names along the sides of the triangle. In particular, have the name of the spirit you wish to invoke. Around the circle have the name Enki to the south, Avalae to the west, Alavarfyn to the north and Tatatyn to the East. You should be the only one in the triangle. Any others should be outside the triangle but within the circle.

(Intone:)

"I OPEN MYS'ELF TO THE TRUTH OF MY BEING. I OPEN MY MIND, MY SOUL, MY BODY AND SPIRIT TO THE RADIANCE OF MY INNER FIRE. I CALL FORTH THE GREAT SNAKE OF THE KUNDALINI TO CLIMB THE STAIRWAY TO HEAVEN THAT RESIDES WITHIN ME, AWAKENING EACH CENTER OF POWER AS IT DOES SO, ILLUMINATING MY ENTIRE BEING. RISE COILED SERPENT OF KNOWLEDGE AND POWER. ARISE, MIGHTY SOURCE OF ETERNAL REGENERATION, AND UNITE ME WITH MY TRUE S'ELF ETERNAL, CASTING AWAY THE VEIL THAT SEPARATES THIS WORLD FROM THE NEXT, THAT DIVIDES THE INNER FROM THE OUTER, SO THAT MY EYES MAY SEE TRULY AND WITHOUT DELUSION THE TOTALITY OF MY UNIVERSE, AND UNDERSTAND IT TO THE DEPTHS OF MY BEING."

(Picking up the Sacred Sacrament say:)

"I NOW UNITE MYS'ELF WITH THE ETERNAL. I SHALL DIE, YET IN DEATH BE BORN TO A NEW AND VASTER REALITY. MY OLD S'ELF SHALL GIVE WAY TO THE NEW AND IN DOING SO FIND ITS PRESERVATION FOR ONLY CHANGE IS CONSTANT AND TRANSFORMATION THE GATEWAY TO IMMORTALITY."

(Now, if you are going to do so, take the Sacred Sacrament.)

"IN ME, IN YOU, IN ALL ETERNITY, THE DIVINE IN ALL THINGS MANIFEST.

"I AM ONE WITH MYS'ELF ETERNAL. I AM ONE WITH THE ETERNAL WITHIN MYS'ELF. I AM ONE ETERNAL. I AM ONE. I AM. IN ALL THINGS I AM MANIFEST. IN ALL THAT I DO, I EXPRESS THE ETERNAL. FROM MY TOUCH COMES PLEASURE. FROM MY VOICE, JOY. FROM MY SMILE, ENCOURAGEMENT. FROM MY LOVE, ECSTASY. IN ALL I DO AND IN ALL I SAY, I CREATE THE WORLD EVERYDAY, AND BORN ANEW EACH MOMENT BRIGHT, AWAKENING TO ETERNAL LIFE."

(Taking up the oil, anoint thys'elf and anyone else present, saying:)

"I DEDICATE MYS'ELF TO TOTAL FULFILLMENT OF MY BODY, MY MIND, MY SOUL AND MY SPIRIT. I ENTER A NEW LIFE IN WHICH MY GENIUS IS UNLEASHED, MY BODY LIBERATED, MY WILL EMPOWERED, AND MY SOUL ELECTRIFIED. MY ENERGY IS BOUNDLESS, AND I AM CAPABLE OF ACHIEVING ANYTHING I DESIRE. I AM IN TUNE WITH MY TRUE DESTINY AND ALL OBSTRUCTIONS GIVE WAY BEFORE ME. ALL THE GOOD THINGS OF LIFE COME TO ME AND I SHARE THEM,

CREATING ABUNDANCE AND PROSPERITY WHEREVER I GO. FROM ALL WHOM I MEET, I LEARN, AND MY KNOWLEDGE OF ALL THINGS INCREASES DAILY. MINE EYES ARE CLEAR AND TO ME ALL THINGS STAND OUT IN THEIR TRUE LIGHT. THERE IS NOTHING THAT IS HIDDEN THAT CANNOT BE REVEALED. THERE IS NO MYSTERY SO PROFOUND THAT EXPLORATION WILL NOT SOLVE IT. YET THERE IS NO END TO MYSTERIES TO BE SOLVED, AND NO END TO THE JOYOUS EXULTATION UPON SOLVING THEM. IN EVERY ACT I BECOME MORE EFFICIENT AND EFFECTIVE, AND MY ABILITIES ARE PERFECTED IN EVERY EFFORT I MAKE."

(Anoint the points of the triangle, each one at a time. Anoint the first point saying:)

"THIS IS THE POINT OF DEVOTION. I SHALL DEVOTE MY LIFE AND ALL MY ENERGY TOWARD THE FULFILLMENT OF MY DREAMS. I SHALL DEVOTE MYS'ELF COMPLETELY AND UTTERLY TO THE REALIZATION OF MY GOALS AND ASPIRATIONS."

(The second point.)

"THIS IS THE POINT OF DISCIPLINE. I SHALL DISCIPLINE MY MIND, MY BODY, AND MY EMOTIONS SO THAT THEIR POWER WILL BE PERFECTED AND WILL RESPOND IMMEDIATELY AND FULLY TO MY WILL. I SHALL DISCIPLINE MYS'ELF SO THAT IN EVERYTHING I DO MY WILL SHALL BE FULFILLED."

(The third point.)

"THIS IS THE POINT OF DESIRE. I DESIRE THAT MY WILL BE FULFILLED IN ALL THINGS, AND THAT MY DESIRES TEMPORARY BE UNITED WITH MY DESIRES ETERNAL. IN ALL THINGS, NO MATTER HOW SMALL, MY WILL SHALL BE FULFILLED AND MY DESIRES HARMONIZE WITH THOSE GOALS THAT ARE INFINITE AND ETERNAL."

(Now, anoint the three sides of the triangle, saying at the first between devotion and discipline:)

"THIS IS THE REALM OF IMMORTALITY. THROUGH DEVOTION AND DISCIPLINE IT SHALL BE ACHIEVED AND I WILL BE UNITED WITH MY ETERNAL SOUL AND SPIRIT, AND MY MIND AND BODY SHALL ACHIEVE IMMORTALITY."

(Second side.)

"THIS IS THE REALM OF ECSTASY, ACHIEVED THROUGH THE UNION OF DISCIPLINE AND DESIRE. IN ALL THINGS I SHALL KNOW JOY AND PLEASURE AND THE BEST OF ALL THINGS SHALL COME TO ME, FULFILLING ME COMPLETELY AND REGENERATING MY BEING."

(Third side.)

"THIS IS THE REALM OF GENIUS, BORN OF THE UNION OF DESIRE AND DEVOTION. I SHALL APPROACH ALL THINGS FROM A FRESH STANDPOINT, AND BE RENEWED AND REFRESHED BY ALL MY EXPERIENCES. I UNITE WITH MY INNER GENIUS AND SHALL OBSERVE ALL THINGS FROM MY OWN PERSPECTIVE, YET SHALL REMAIN OPEN TO ALL

OTHER VIEWS SO THAT IN ALL I ENCOUNTER I WILL LEARN, GROW AND EXPAND MY KNOWLEDGE AND EXPERIENCE.

"I AM OPEN. I AM READY. LET MY SPIRIT AND BODY UNITE. LET MY MIND AND SOUL MERGE. NOW!"

(Lift up your arms and allow the Spirit to fill you. When you are ready take up the book of spells.)

"I SHALL WRITE A NEW BOOK OF MAGIC BASED ON MY OWN EXPERIENCE, RESEARCH AND UNDERSTANDING THAT OTHERS MIGHT TAKE IT AND FIND THE PATHWAY TO THEIR MAGIC AND IN TIME EACH SPIRIT SHALL BE FULFILLED COMPLETELY, ACCORDING TO ITS OWN NATURE, DESTINY, DESIRES AND PROPENSITIES.

"I CREATE A NEW MAGIC AND WITH IT A NEW WORLD, A WORLD IN WHICH ALL BEINGS WILL FIND THE FULFILLMENT THEY SEEK SHOULD THEY BUT SEEK IT.

"I GIVE BIRTH TO A NEW AGE OF MIRACLES WHEREIN ALL THINGS ARE POSSIBLE, BORN OF DEVOTION, DISCIPLINE AND DESIRE. IMMORTALITY, ECSTASY AND GENIUS SHALL BE OURS, AND WE WILL BE UNITED IN LOVE FOREVER, UNLOCKING THE MYSTERIES OF LIFE.

"SO I SAY. SO SHALL IT BE. NOW AND FOREVER MORE IN TIME ETERNAL AND SPACE INFINITE."

(Now go to the northern point of the triangle and have your Divine consort take up the crown and say:)

"YOU ARE MY GOD (DESS) AND I AM YOUR GOD (DESS). YOU ARE THE PRINCE (SS) OF MY LIFE, THE JOY OF MY HEART, THE SUBJECT OF MY DESIRE AND THE INSPIRATION OF MY BEING. I AM AWAKENED IN YOU AS YOU AWAKE IN

108

ME AND TOGETHER WE ASCEND TO EVER-GREATER
HEIGHTS OF OUR DESTINY. I CROWN YOU, CREATOR
DIVINE, LOVER MINE, SPIRIT OF THE SACRED TRINE."

(Place the crown on hir head.)

"YOU ARE MY INSPIRATION. YOU ARE MY GUIDE. IN YOU I
AM REBORN. IN YOU I WILL RESIDE FOREVER MORE."

(Now the Crowned One speaks, saying:)

"WE LOVE YOU. WE LOVE YOU ALL. YOU HAVE OUR
BLESSING AND PROTECTION. WE AUTHORIZE YOU TO RISE
AS WE HAVE, TO STAND AS AN EQUAL AMONG THE
RADIANT STAR BEINGS. RISE UP, LOVED ONES. AWAKEN
TO A NEW LIFE IN A NEW REALM OF OUR CREATION. BY
OUR POWERS ALL THINGS ARE MADE ANEW AND TOGETHER
ALL THINGS BECOME POSSIBLE. WE ARE WITH YOU NOW
AND FOREVER MORE, AND IF EVER YOU NEED US YOU NEED
BUT CALL OUT AND OUR MAGIC WILL REACH OUT TO YOU.
OUR SPIRITS SHALL BE ONE IN ETERNITY AND WE SHALL
DANCE AMONG THE STARS ECSTATIC IN OUR DIVINITY,
AWAKENED TO THE TRUE LIFE IMMORTAL. GROWING EVER
MORE CONSCIOUSLY INTELLIGENT. UNITING WITH THE ALL
OF LIFE. AWARE OF THE PARTS, AS WELL AS THE
TOTALITY. OVERLOOKING NOTHING. OUR BENEFICENCE
SPREADS UNHINDERED IN ALL DIRECTIONS, WITHIN AND
WITHOUT, ON EARTH AND IN SPACE, INNER AND OUTER,
AD INFINITUM.

"ENKI, MY BROTHER, AVALAE MY SISTER, WE JOIN YOU IN
YOUR QUEST TO FREE THE MINDS, BODIES, SPIRITS AND
SOULS OF ALL BEINGS. IN OUR UNION, OUR POWERS ARE

INVINCIBLE. OF OUR UNION ARE BORN NEW GENERATIONS OF WILLING ACCOMPLICES IN THE GREAT ADVENTURE OF UNLOCKING THE MYSTERIES OF THE UNIVERSE.

"UNITED FOREVER IN LOVE TOGETHER, GROWING SMARTER AND SMARTER IN EVERY MOMENT THAT PASSES. IN US ARE UNITED THE FUTURE, THE PAST, AND THE PRESENT, AND THOUGH US ALL THINGS COME TO BE. TOGETHER FOREVER IN LOVE.

"SO WE HAVE SPOKEN. SO IT IS. SO SHALL IT BE, NOW AND FOREVER MORE. ECSTASY ETERNAL. LIVE PARADISE NOW!

"LIVE PARADISE NOW!

"LIVE PARADISE NOW!"

(Seal the circle and go forth into a new realm of being.)

CHAPTER 6:

USING MUDRAS AND TATTOOS

IN MAGIC

Mudras are hand positions, and finger intertwining, used in magical workings and meditations to help unite and focus the will, body and consciousness toward a desired goal. To attain what you will in magic, you must will it with your entire being. If you are split in your desire, both wanting it and not wanting it, you are blocking yours'elf. If you are weak in your desire, wanting it, but not enough, you will be unlikely to get it, or it will take such a long time you'll probably have forgotten it by the time it comes. Mudras help you focus all your attention toward the desired end. In this way, your power is enhanced and the vibration of your "sending" is both pure and strong. Mudras help get your body into the act, so to speak. Your mind is focused, your feelings elevated and ecstatically embracing the magic, your will and intent clear, and your body with the use of mudras and/or resonated spells/chants give a base, a center, for your enchantment.

In the following pages, we describe those that may be drawn upon for use with each of the color magics. There are many more than these; however, these will suffice to begin with. While the mudras are effective when used in a magic ceremony or ritual, they can also be utilized at nearly anytime, such as when you are waiting for an appointment, etc., or even during communication and interchanges with others. The mudra allows you to focus your mind and will at any particular instant, quickly and effectively.

In some magics, tattoos, even temporary tattoos such as you would have with the use of henna, may be used to enchant/enspell/ensorcel the body. Some eastern magicians have Buddhists sutras tattooed on their bodies. Those elves of a Celtic lineage may wish to have Celtic knots and swirls. The elf may wish to paint the glyph for the spirits that are being evoked or invoked. Or may wish to paint, draw the spell its'elf, written in Arvyndase (see *Arvyndase: a Short Course in the Language of the Silver Elves*) or some other elven or magical script, such as Angelic or Enochian. (For advanced magicians, we recommend David Allen Hulse's *The Key to It All*, book 2:*The Western Mysteries* for great tables of correspondence.)

Of course, one doesn't need to get a permanent tattoo, unless they so desire, and even henna will take weeks to fade, so if you are placing the tattoos on your face or hands, you may wish to use markers that can be easily washed off. Watercolors often work well for face paints but will crack and peal on their own. In our experience, a bit of face cream added to the paint will help it stay vibrant and flexible. You can also use theatrical paints if you have them, since they are made to endure on the face even under intense light. Or you could even use ink pens. This may be a bit harder to wash off, so you may wish to experiment on a small area first.

While such tattooing helps bring the physical body into the magic and can also help create the proper atmosphere for the magic, the intonation of the spells and the use of the mudras are, we think, even more important since they are an active, rather than passive, part of the magic. It is the mudras and chants that bring the tattoos to life and make them glow throughout the planes and dimensions with the magic. On the physical plane they may look to be but ink (unless you paint them with fluorescent paint and enact your magic in the dark), but on the higher, or more subtle, planes of manifestation they will glow with a magical radiance, the light of Elfin/Faerie shining through you.

Purity: White Magic

The mudra for purity has one open hand – fingers together, covering the top of the other. When the hands are palms up, with one open hand resting in the palm of the other hand, it indicates that one has cleansed ones'elf and is open to receiving guidance, inspiration, etc. from the universe. The hands in this position are cupped slightly, as if to capture water, but also to bring to mind the image of one hand washing the other.

If in doing this, one feels the influx of Universal energy, or the radiance of Faerie, one can, when sHe feels sHe has received as much as has been sent, or as much as sHe can handle at that time, turn the top hand over so the palms are facing each other. This is the sign of absorption. Cup this energy gently, like one would a small bird held in one's hands. One is letting the energetic message or gift be absorbed by one's being. It helps if one inhales the energy while doing this. Visualize it going through your palms, up your arms, spreading through your body, and then radiating outward through your aura. Let the spirit of Elfin manifest though you. You make Elfin real as you realize Elfin.

One can reverse this position and have the hands, one over the other, palms downward. In this position, one is indicating that sHe is in the process of cleaning hirs'elf, or preparing to do so, but is not yet ready to catch the gaze of the universal power, and desires time and protection to make things right, or make amends. In effect, one is saying: "Let me take care of this. I'll resolve this problem before there is a need for Karmic retribution." Or, "I know I have Karmic debts and I am in the process of paying them." Unlike banks or loan sharks to whom one owes ever more the longer to one takes to pay off one's debt, the Magic is very lenient and forgiving of those who are actively in the process of setting things right. One's guardian angels, the Shining Ones, who are the elven who have progressed or evolved higher in the supra-dimensional realms, have one's back, so to speak if one is sincerely making an effort. We can count on our elfin kith and kin to aide us as we progress ever further into Elfin.

Retribution: Black Magic

The mudra for the black magic consists of two closed fists shoved together, knuckles to knuckles, in front of your chest with your fingers toward your chest. This position brings things to a head. It forces a situation and instigates conflict. It says that you are ready to defend yours'elf with force and in some cases moves your opponent to act before sHe is fully prepared. It is meant to intimidate and cower your enemy and to convey to them psychologically that they cannot win against you, and might as well give up, or retreat permanently.

Reversed, with the backs of your fists toward your chest, it promotes conflict among your enemies and does not involve you at all. In this fashion, you give your opponents a psychological propensity for fighting among themselves, thus constantly weakening them from within. It promotes confusion among them and keeps them from ever organizing a successful attack. Their attention and powers become constantly distracted, and they dissipate their energy before they can make a move against you. It also calls the wrath of the universe upon them and hastens their karma. Each or any of these events should be visualized while doing this mudra.

However, the last part, the calling of Karma should only be used if you are karmically free of having caused this conflict, for when you call karma down on others, you are inevitably calling it down on yours'elf as well. This is to say your are asking the Lypyca Lords, the Lords of Karma to examine the lives of your opponents, however, to do so you must be open to having your own karma examined as well. That is just the way it is. Just as you can't look into another's eyes, and soul, without them being able to look back into your eyes and soul;

so, too, you can't call down the Lords of Karma without attracting their notice. As we say, use this power carefully.

Another position, involves one fist upward and the other downward, knuckles against each other. This position pushes one's opponent toward compromise. They begin to feel they cannot win in the conflict and have to compromise with you. Use this only if you have to stay involved with the individual in some fashion. Otherwise, you may wish to use one of the positions that compels them to withdrawal and thus remove themselves from your life. Remember, also, that in using this position you will have to compromise as well. It is not just a matter of them surrendering, but of you coming to an agreement with them that will end the conflict.

Remember, too, that ending a conflict is just the beginning. Having someone withdrawal from your life and realm is also only a partial solution. The ultimate goal is always the positive evolution of the soulful spirit of each individual; so once a compromise has been reached, or the person has departed from your life, remember to send hir a blessing to help hir on hir way to hir true path and destiny. The best way to end conflict is to have each individual find hir own true place in the Universe. If the individual is pursuing hir true path, she won't be interfering with yours.

Healing: Green Magic

The mudra for healing others is done by having the palms outward, the fingers together and the thumbs touching at the tips. This is the same hand position, individually or both hands together, that you may use for caressing and healing someone's aura, moving your hands over, but not touching their body. It can also be used effectively in direct contact with the ailing area. Often, when one is finished, the hands are flicked to cast off any negative influences with which they may have come in contact. They may also feel very warm when the energy is passing through them.

For s'elf healing, the hands are turned with the palms toward your body, fingers still together, hands crossed at the wrists and thumbs crossed and pressing against each other. The hands can also be used individually on the effected area, consciously channeling the power of healing into that spot.

For the most part, it is good to use the left hand on the right side of the body and the right on the left, since the side of the body that is ailing is best healed by the side that is well. You can also place one hand on the place that is hurting and the other on the spot where you feel strongest, channeling the energy from wellness into the illness.

In distance healing, the individual is touched through the imaginal planes. That is you visualize the individual, or hear their voice, or in some other way arouse your memory of them, and putting out your hands as previously indicated, send them healing. (You may wish to read Diane Stein's *Essential Reiki*.)

Prosperity: Orange Magic

The Orange Magic mudra consists of having the left hand cup the right from below. The right hand is turned palm upward with the thumb, index and middle finger held together and the ring and little finger folded inward to the palm. The thumb, index and middle fingers can also be rubbed together as in the traditional symbol for money. Use this mudra to attract money and resources to you. The right hand, with the fingers rubbing, attracts the prosperity, while the left hand that cups it is the receptive hand. It symbolizes the opening into which the prosperity will flow. In this way, the cupped hand is related to the Chalice and the suit of cups in the Tarot. The right hand with its rubbing fingers, like rubbing sticks together to start a fire, is associated with the suit of Wands.

By reversing the mudra and cupping the left hand with the right, you can direct energy toward others who need financial success. This position can also be effective for helping you, or someone else, learn how to distribute wealth effectively. Remember the key to financial success is not simply to accumulate wealth (ultimately gathering is always followed by dispersal) but to keep it circulating. The best way is to distribute while you are accumulating, which helps balance out and prevent inflation, recession cycles, and upheavals caused by poverty and monetary cycles of depression. The association between financial periods of depression and psychological depression is not accidental. Poverty can be very depressing. Keep in mind that money is like water, it must flow and be kept in motion or the economy will stagnate.

Mudras are a form of evocation. Use them often to keep the flow going. Magic, like money, is a form of energy. It, too, must be kept circulating. Like your body, the magic must be exercised regularly to keep it in peak condition. By stretching the magic, by trying to do a little more each time, you extend your powers and capabilities. However, do this slowly. Just as you don't wish to overextend yours'elf financially, you also do not wish to overreach with your magic.

If you have enough for yours'elf financially but wish to improve the flow of money in general and among your others, do the finger rubbing money symbol with both hands. The money will not flow directly to you, but it will stimulate the economy in general. If you wish to slow down inflation, do this same mudra with your hands turned downward.

Remember, money to the elves is not a competition about winning and having when others don't have and thus lose. To us, the more each of us has, the more all of us have. Money is not a pie we cut up and share and there are only so many pieces to go around. Money is a crop we plant and harvest, over and over again. Money is indeed a tree we've planted that blossoms regularly and bears fruit. The magic money tree is an elfin tree.

It is our family tree, which blossoms as we share and help each other. Normals say money doesn't grow on trees, but it does in Elfin.

Opportunity, Creativity: Purple Magic

Press your palms and fingers together, fingers and thumbs spread wide. This mudra symbolizes many paths coming together, thus many opportunities. It is symbolizes that we all come from One Source, which is The Magic, and no matter how much we may diversify, differentiate, or go our separate ways we are always connected to and a part of that Source. It reminds us of the paradox that we are both unique and therefore the same, or the same in our uniqueness. You can use this mudra to create job opportunities, as well as enhance your creative potential. This is like the position many folks use for praying, but with the fingers spread rather than together.

Alternately, you can do this mudra with palms together, thumbs crossed and fingers side by side pointed upward but pressed together on their sides, much like the traditional pose for praying except that the fingers are interlaced side to side inside of flat against each other. This method of using the mudra is particularly good for creating unusual or alternative possibilities. It symbolizes many pathways of equal value, thus it also promotes mutual tolerance. However this does not mean they come together or are alike, except in their agreement to disagree. This mudra will help in finding new pathways, or gaining acceptance for a new path.

This mudra is effective for researchers as well as creative artists of all sorts. Whatever you do, or whatever you really want to do to make money, if you truly believe in it then do it, and this mudra will help you succeed both as an artist/scientist and as a member of society. Pursue your goals wholeheartedly and time will show that nature made you to be just as you are. However, this requires acceptance of others and their paths as well. As our blessed Mother always told us, "You have to accept people for who they are."

Love, Romance, Sex: Red Magic

Put your left hand in front of you, fingers together, thumb extended upward at a right angle to the fingers, palm toward your chest. Now, grasp the thumb with your right hand, bending the right thumb around it from the inside at the base and closing the fingers of the right hand around it from the outside with the right thumb over the fingers of the right hand, so you have the right first enclosing the left thumb. Now, close the fingers of the left hand around the thumb of the right hand, so now your have two closed fists with their thumbs interlocked and touching the index finger of its own hand.

This is the mudra for attracting love and sex to you. Reverse the hand if you wish (that is put the left hand on top) to put the emphasis on romance and affection. If, instead of romance or sex, you wish to create friendship between yours'elf and others, or if you wish to limit someone who desires you romantically to a relationship of friendship, you can use the following mudra.

Put your hands into fists, except for the index fingers, which are hooked to each other. This is the American Sign Language for the deaf symbol for friend and used as a mudra helps create friendship.

Keep in mind that the place where you use the mudra is also important. If, for instance, you take martial arts and you do the mudra for money, or this one for sex/romance, in the dojo, it indicates that you wish money or sex to come to you through the dojo. So use the mudra in the place where you wish the desired object, subject or goal to manifest.

An alternate mudra for attracting a sexual relationship is to take the middle finger, often called the bird, or the fuck you finger, and encompass it with the other hand. And while it may seem crude, moving the finger in and out of the hand to stimulate sex is such a commonly used mudra that it has taken on the power of frequent use and recognition. This will attract sexual energy to you, although this tends to attract relationships that emphasis sex over friendship, which from an elven point of view is not always wise. We nearly always believe friendship to be the underlying basis of all relationships and without friendship sex can leave one feeling empty. And the sex itself seems meaningless. Also, such relationships often pass quickly, so one is ever looking for more of them, and when they end they often turn very negative. Yet, as we mentioned, the mudra is a very common one, in frequently use, although usually used as a sign of communication rather than a magical mudra, and it has power, thus we mention it here. Using the middle finger of the right hand symbolizes seeking sex. Using the middle finger of the left hand indicates drawing it to you.

Some may find this mudra too crude for their use, and we sympathize. These elves do not make such judgments. To us it is merely a mudra and its common use, while crude, does not mean we have to use it crudely ours'elves, which is to say in public while winking and/or making strange lascivious facial expressions. On the other hand, we are not inclined toward casual relationships, at least at this point in our lives. The Stars know we had more than a few in our youth, and most of them were great. Still, an underlying spiritual communion is always desired by these elves even in relationships where the sex is, or has been, casual.

Alternately, if you wish to ensure friendship along with a sexual relationship, do the same mudra but interlink the index fingers, as in the friendship mudra, as you do so. Again, the right middle finger in the left hand symbolizes wanting signs or omens to guide you toward the relationship, and the left middle finger denotes drawing the relationship to you in the places you tend to go (and where you do the mudra).

Wisdom: Blue Magic

The mudra for the blue magic has the two hands coming together, palms toward your chest, ends of the fingers interlocked and thumbs upward at a 90° angle to the fingers. This position is an invocation of knowledge and wisdom. You are calling wisdom down into your being. The interlocked fingers symbolize the integration of the knowledge you receive.

By bringing the thumbs together, it becomes a mudra for concentrating your mind and your will, and particularly for using the knowledge you have in a wise, effective and efficient way.

By crossing the thumbs, it becomes the mudra for silence, for keeping and preserving the mysteries and revealing them only to those who are ready for initiation. Whereas, by opening the hands so the palms are upward, the thumbs away from you and the fingers intertwined, but not hooked together, it becomes the mudra for the dissemination of information, the spreading of the word.

While you can usually use a mudra in most situations, there could be times when it may not be possible, for whatever reason, to do so. In such a case, it is possible to visualize the mudra, doing it thus on the mental/imaginal planes, which can also be effective. Remember the imaginal planes are the plans, the architectural and archetypal designs, upon which the world is created.

These mudras can be used in a general way toward accumulating knowledge of all sorts, or for summoning whatever knowledge and/or secrets the universe deems appropriate at the time to reveal to you. It can also be used in a more specific fashion toward attaining knowledge on a particular subject or technique. It can be used to reveal the hidden, as well as improve your ability in any desired area in which you seek greater knowledge and understanding.

However, there may be things we are not yet developed enough to comprehend. In these cases, like a child hearing something that doesn't make sense to hir at the time, we can only store the essence of the information for the future when understanding will suddenly dawn on us, and what seemed obscure becomes clear through revelation. The Mysteries are often revealed like a jigsaw puzzle. We fit together numerous pieces giving us glimpses and hints until finally we get a sense of what the overall picture is.

These mudras of the Blue Magic can also be used to increase one's intelligence, which is to say clear the mind so it works more effectively and efficiently. It can also open the mind to inspiration so new, powerful, and transformative ideas can easily enter in. Note that there is more than one type of intelligence. Howard Gardner theorizes there are at least 9 types of intelligence, including musical intelligence, natural intelligence, and social intelligence (see *Frames of Mind. The theory of multiple intelligences* by Howard Gardner). All of these different forms of intelligence can be increased and made more powerful through the use of these mudras.

Harmony and Peace: Yellow Magic

If you wish to instigate peace and harmony among people who are not predisposed to harmonizing with each other, use this mudra. Bring the fists together, one up and one down, and so the knuckles are against each other then extend the thumbs so each one rests on the little finger of the opposite hand by crossing it's own index finger. Have the right hand thumb on top if you wish to emphasize logic and reason over passion, and the left thumb to the top if you wish to emphasize affection and passion over ideology and rationalization.

To bring peace to those who are bickering, but do not hate each other, and in fact may be naturally inclined toward harmony, have each hand grasp the wrist of the other hand.
122

Again, have the right or left hand, thumb up, depending on which powers you wish to emphasize.

Logic and reason are good when people dislike or hate each other, but where their financial or other common interests can bring them together. Alternately, where the source of conflict is one of ideology and philosophy, the emphasis will be on affection and feeling since we must arouse the feeling of love for one's own group to spare it the pain and suffering of conflict, and the feelings of sympathy to put one in another's shoes, so to speak.

Another mudra that is effective for bringing together those who have minor disagreements, is to have one had grasp the other as though you are shaking your own hand, only with one hand over the other. This one is not so effective for major disagreements. This mudra can also be used when you are about to meet someone for the first time and you wish to create an atmosphere of harmony prior to the meeting. Again whether the right hand is up or the left depends upon which aspect, logic or feeling, you wish to emphasis. Also, note that for individuals who are left-handed this sequence may vary. Use your own intuition to determine which way represents the logical and which the feeling aspect.

These mudras can be used on a small scale, such as one's own family, coven, group, etc. or on a vast scale, as in promoting world peace and harmony. If the response to your workings isn't immediately apparent that need not worry you. In the astral planes you can snap your fingers and anything you want or think will occur instantly. But the world of matter is the world of space/time, thus all magics must unravel through space/time, out and back again to manifest. In your mind a newborn baby can be instantly a child, a teenager, or an adult, but in space/time changes are not instantaneous, but sequential. Here the phenomena of cause and effect come into play, and it is exactly this phenomenon that makes magic possible on the material world.

Remember, contrary to what most people believe, magic is not a violation of Nature, or of the natural order, but is achieved through a greater understanding of the nature of reality. Magic does not violate the laws of Nature, but uses them to achieve its ends. (Which does not mean we don't stretch the rules now and again.) However, reality is far vaster and infinitely more flexible, more protean, than most folks comprehend. We elves love Nature and achieve our magic by harmonizing with it, becoming one with it, and making it our friend, not by going around it, above it, or forcing it. You might say magic comes naturally to the elves.

Evocation, Initiation, The Quickening: Gold Magic Mudras

Bring your hands together and cross them at the wrists with the thumbs interlocked and the palms toward you, the fingers splayed like wings. Now, fold and interlock the fingers around the thumbs. This is the gold magic mudra, and it will aid you in influencing a particular person/spirit to come and appear before you, or contact you. If your relationship with them is basically one of business, such as a contract to be fulfilled, then have the right wrist closer to you and the right thumb over the left. If your relationship is one that is more feeling and emotional/personal in nature, have the left wrist toward you and the left thumb on top.

By placing this mudra against your forehead or heart, or some other chakra position, it becomes the mudra for "the quickening". (The chakra position being the primary influence for how the quickening functions. Thus concerns about survival in the world would involve first/base chakra and so on.) These positions, especially the 5th, 6th, and 7th chakra positions, promote and instigate change, and move you rapidly toward your next initiation. Use this mudra carefully because the consequences can be quite severe if you are not really ready to move on. Keep in mind that turning up the heat doesn't necessarily make the cake bake quicker, it can burn it. You may be calling too much force upon yours'elf, but as in all things Seelie Elfin, you must be the judge.

This mudra can also be used to "quicken" others. In this case, extend the mudra outward so the hands are away from the body and the elbows against your abdomen. This also should be done with care, and in most instances it is unwise to use it as a weapon. However, doing so might harm the individual by increasing hir power beyond hir ability to handle it (although it is a very clever and elven way of proceeding, but has its risks). It could just backfire on you, for sHe may prove more resilient than you think, and you will have lent hir power instead of having hampered hir. Also, and this is the clever part, it has the consequence, karmically, of increasing your own power when the energy comes back to you. But, remember that the intention is an important part of magic so if your intention was to overload the person that intention will also return to you. Plus, the energy returning to you will be amplified/multiplied, as it always is in magic, and thus what may have been an overload for that individual could be an extreme overload for you, even if you are very advanced in regard to your opponent. Again, the vital aspect in magic, particularly as you rise in the supra-dimensional spiritual planes of being and the deeper realms of Faerie, is intention. Thus when Jesus advised us to love our enemies, he was being a very clever, knowledgeable and wise elf, indeed.

Thus, even when your intentions are good, you would be wise to exercise caution in using this mudra. Are you sure you are helping them? Are you ready to assume the responsibility for making that judgment? All magic returns to its creator. All elfin magic returns with stardust.

Invocation, The Ascension:
Silver Magic Mudra

The mudra for the silver magic helps you to ascend to new and higher levels of being. Here you do not wait for initiation, you initiate. You assume responsibility for your own life and power, and the use of those powers. You are a pioneer in unexplored territory, and you create your own pathway. You begin to transform the raw potentiality of the Magic, which is at the heart of the Universe, and shape it as you Will to create your own realm of Faerie/Elfin according to your Vision.

For this mudra, bring your hands together so your thumbs, index fingers, and little fingers are touching at the tips. Your ring and middle fingers should be touching at the knuckles along the length of the middle digits.

Or, you can create your own mudra for this position. Can you? Do you dare? If you do, will you believe in it, and use it, and be empower by it? Or do you need to see it in a book to believe in it? That is the real question. Do you dare create your own world, your own magic, your own mudra? If not, then you're not really ready for this level of power. However, if that is the case, the mudra we described above will help you to prepare for this level. Do it until you are ready, or are inspired to create your own. This is the transition point. You can do it. We have complete confidence in you. After all, you are a spiritual descendant of the Elven-Faerie peoples.

Ultimately, you can't get your magic from books. This book's one true purpose is to encourage you to do your own elfin magic. Everything we write and do here is merely presented as examples for you to learn by, to mix and match, transform into your own, in your personal style, motivated by your personal power. We elves are both eclectic concerning our magic and our culture, and transformative. We take everything we find, like, love, and to which we feel a relation, and we make it our own. We elfinize it. We wave our magic wands over it, sprinkle it with faery dust, pixie powder, and starlight and it becomes elven. We encourage you to do the same in your own way.

And we trust that you in turn will aid others to do the same, until all of us have been freed, our powers unleashed, and paradise/Elfin/Faerie reclaimed. It is ours after all, our home, our culture, and our creation.

We speak to you across time/space, setting this magic in motion so that when we come again these words, or others like them, will help us toward the liberation of our minds, bodies, souls and spirits. Just think, we could be your children, your grandchildren, your sister, brother, cousin, friend, or kin; we could even be you!

CHAPTER 7:

USING MANTRAS IN MAGIC

Mantras are short chants of one or a few words that can be repeated over and over again to attune one's consciousness, and thus move one's universe/being toward the fulfillment of one's will. The mantras that follow are used most effectively in conjunction with the specified mudra, discussed in the last chapter.

White Magic

1. All things cleansed, all things clear. Open heart, open mind, clear way.

2. Time for rectifying my errors.

3. The Way opens.

4. Everything is becoming ever more clear.

Black Magic

1. I am strong. I am ready. Now is the time.

2. Obstruction, confusion, my enemies disillusioned.

3. I'm not here. You do not see me. You attention goes elsewhere.

Green Magic

1. Healing is contagious; pass it around.

2. Within, without and all about, I am healthy and well.

3. Energized, actualized, ever getting better.

Orange Magic

1. Prosperity is mine, now and for all time.
2. There is plenty for everyone.
3. We have all we need and more to share.

Purple Magic

1. All doors open before me; I am free to choose my way.
2. Many paths, many ways, to each their own on every day.
3. My own way in my own time.

Red Magic

1. The heat of your passion increases each day, drawing you closer to me in all ways.
2. The depth of our feeling is gentle and pure; candlelight, moonlight and walks by the shore.
3. Our friendship increases each moment to pass; a friendship enduring and strong that will last.
4. Ever closer we become.

Blue Magic

1. All knowledge is mine; I open my mind.
2. I focus my mind and all that I desire comes true.

3. The Mysteries are preserved in me.

4. The truth revealed, proclaims itself.

5. All I seek ... revealed.

6. Every secret yields to my hunger for truth.

Yellow Magic

1. Peace is profitable.

2. Peace is the only logical solution.

3. There is no alternative but peace.

4. With all my heart and all my soul, I embrace peace.

5. For the sake of the children, we must have peace.

6. There is no future without peace.

7. As we work together the world flourishes.

Gold Magic

1. I invite you to manifest here and now, for our mutual advantage and prosperity.

2. My soul reaches out and calls you to me with each heartbeat.

3. I am ready and am entering a new and vaster realm of experience and power.

4. I initiate your evolution and all things hasten to be fulfilled.

5. Come to me, come to me, come to me now. (also works with Red Magic Mudra)

Silver Magic

1. I can do it. I can do it. I can do it.

2. Yes, yes, yes.

3. All I Will ... will be.

4. Create your own mantras.

While the mantras and mudras are quite simple, they are individually and together immensely powerful. The fact that they can be done at nearly any time will help you to extend and interweave the magic through the fabric of your mundane life, thus turning routine into power filled ritual. This will have the effect of stabilizing your magic while transforming your routine. In the course of time, the boring will be trans-mutated into the joyous and the mundane elements that may have been "getting you down" will become the base and support for the actualization of your Will.

Remember, mantras can be done silently, and mudras surreptitiously whenever you are sitting around waiting for an appointment, or riding the bus, or otherwise in a situation where nothing seems to be going on except waiting. Instead of feeling impatient, do your mantras and mudras and set your magic in motion. Feed your magic. Transform frustration into an act of energizing your will.

Mantras can also be done while one goes about completing mundane chores. Sweeping, vacuuming, or doing the dishes can be turned into a White Magic Ritual. This is particularly effective if one feels their magic is stagnating, or one has come to a stalemate and nothing seems to be happening. Cooking can be spiced with Red Magic, Orange Magic, Green Magic, or other magics, or combinations of magic. Use your imagination and make your life and every moment magical.

Part Two:

Directions and Dimensions

in Magic

CHAPTER 8:

THE FOUR DIRECTIONS

While it is common in rituals these days to make evocations in the four directions: North, East, South and West, in a certain sense there are really only two directions in magic: Inward and Outward, what is within the magic circle, or really sphere, and everything beyond its perimeters. We might compare this idea to Jung's (Psychological Types) notion that each of us has a basic personality inclination to approach life as an Introvert or an Extravert, while Crowley in *Magic Without Tears* proffered the opinion that Yoga was an essentially introverted path and Magic an extraverted one.

There is a magical dictum As Above; So Below, this is, in the opinion of these elves, based on an ancient view that Heaven exists above Earth. These elves say rather As Within; So Without or As Within; So Beyond, that is what is without or beyond the Magic Circle reflects what's within the Circle; which is why, for these elves at least, our magic is nearly always based on the premise that in order to transform the world and our circumstances within it, we must first transform our own s'elves. We extend to this the idea that Elfin/Faerie is born of our being and that the world at large is a reflection, however dim or misty, of Elfin/Faerie.

The four directions are a terrestrial convenience, born as it were from our tendency to navigate on an Earth that, despite what we know to the contrary, appears to be more or less flat. In space travel, this simplified navigational system would include not only the four directions as forward, backward, right and left, but also up and down, and we have known some who include this more comprehensive understanding in their rituals. However, because we most often draw our magic circles on relatively flat surfaces, the illusion of flatness and thus the four directions, is reinforced, and paradoxically, it is our magical imagination, as well as our knowledge of the truth of reality, that helps us overcome this terrestrial mirage.

One of the difficulties with attaching meaning to the four directions is a tendency to derive these meanings from our sense of the seasons, that is North is often associated with Winter and a time of reflection, and South associated with Summer and fiery activity. The problem with these attributions is that they are utterly reversed in the Southern Hemisphere where Summer and warmer weather is to the North (where the Equator is), so to speak, and Winter, from the South or the South Pole. Thus it seems to these elves that while we accept the convenience of evoking the four quarters, and that while we could simply reverse the meaning of associations depending upon whether we're on the Northern or Southern Hemisphere, it might be more convenient to develop meanings for the directions that have Planetary application. However, if we detach the South from fiery summer, with what do we associate it?

These elves propose to relate the directions to the five mystic centers of Faery. According to the Murrays in the *Celtic Tree Oracle* there is Falias to the North, Finias to the South, Gorias to the East and Marius to the West, and with ever an acknowledgment of that greater reality of Within and Without, we have the magic circle itself, which is also one's Eald, a central dot or circle at the heart of Elfin/Faerie.

These four outer directions are associated with the four treasures of the Sidhe (pronounced She, the ancient Faery Folk of Eire), the Stone of Fal, which screams (we prefer sings) when the true King sits upon it, the Spear of Lugh, that grants victory to whomever holds it (as we've noted previously these elves also relate this is the spear and staff of Odin), the Sword of Nuada, that cannot be escaped, and the Cauldron of Daghda, from which no one leaves hungry. Anderson in *The*

Celtic Oracles drawing from *The Book of Invasions* calls them Goirras, Findas, Muiras and Failius. These elves for our own part give them our own Elven names based on the primarily vowels of our Aelfabet: Avalan to the West, Elfynea in the Center, Intyrnalys in the East, Ovyryn in the North, and Uvynde to the South.

We will relate Avalan with the Cauldron, which would also be the Cup in the Tarot, usually associated with water, community and relationships. It is also the Chalice, the Holy Grail, both as a Chalice and as the bloodline of the elves. (See Laurence Gardner *Realm of the Ring Lords*).

Intyrnalys (pronounced eye - ter - nah - liss) we will connect with the Sword of Nuada, obviously related to Swords in the Tarot suits, Air, knowledge, and intellect; but also associated with Athame, the trowel, the plough, etc. Some might find it curious that the Sword, which is usually related to warrior principles of combat, would also be associated with farming, gardening, etc. but tradition, both popular and mythic, connects them through time. Note the saying, from the Christian Bible, of turning your swords into Plowshares. But we might also note that Mars/Aries, before he was the God of War, was the God of Fertility. Also, the Chinese God Kuan Ti is both the God of War, as protector and defender of the Realm, but also the God of Prosperity (see Christie, *Chinese Mythology*). Note also that the *I Ching* states that only a people who are secure and prosperous can be an effective support in a war situation, thus the obligation of rulers would always be, first and foremost, the protection and prosperity of the common people.

The sword is a symbol of choice, and a choice between War and Prosperity is an easy one, at least for these elves. Although Dominator societies put forth the idea that the way to prosperity is through war, that is to say prosperity is achieved through conquering others, enslaving their populations and stealing their resources. This is, however, a parasitic approach to life, rather than a symbiotic approach. We elves always endeavor to create symbiotic relationships with all beings. This is also the difference between what are called Zero Sum games, one person wins and all others lose, and Win-Win situations. Seelie Elves always strive to create circumstances in which each and everyone wins/gains.

To the North and Ovyryn (Oh - ver - ren) we assign the Stone of Fal, related to the Pentacles/Coins in the Tarot, to Earth, to the Shield and clearly to the magic circle itself, which is to say the aura of the Realm, what these elves call our Eald on the gross material plane, what most people think of as reality. The fact that the Stone of Fal sings when the true king sits upon it is symbolic of the fact that the Earth, or a particular Eald or Realm, knows/chooses its own King/Queen. The ancient association between the rulers and nature, or the land, is very much a part of Elven Tradition.

In the South, Uvynde (you - vin - dee) we have the Spear of Lug/Lugh the Lord of light, associated with fire, the Staff (Wizard,) in the Tarot the Wand (will power) and for elves, the arrow (travel and communication over distances) or the dart, the elf shot.

At the very center we place Elfynea (L - fin - knee - ah) associated with Ether, spirit and the realms and powers invisible, symbolic of the fact that we are a hidden people and are only truly known by those in the inner circle, thus an indication of the esoteric heart of Elfin magic. Traditionally, there is no treasure associated with the center, however, by its nature the treasures associated with it would be the Ring of Power, symbolizing the union of the Elven Peoples, and the Magic Mirror, through which one sees the future or any part of the realm. The Ring of Power would be like the Ring in the Lord of the Rings only forged for positive spiritual purposes of evolution and enlightenment, rather than dominance and control over others. The Magic Mirror is naturally associated with the Mirror of Galadriel, which was a pool of water, indicating that at the center of Elfin springs forth the Sacred Pool of Healing and Immortality.

We notice that if we accept these attributions that we have come again to the tradition with the North related to Earth, East to Air, South to Fire, and West to Water. We would also note that there is some overlap (as really there should be) of the concepts, as for instance, the fact that the Cauldron represents abundance and wisdom, even though the traditional symbol of wealth and material success in the Tarot would be the Stone/Pentacles/Coins. However, this derives from the fact that to the elves, wisdom dictates that true wealth comes from community and sharing, as opposed to being hidden and buried under rocks, as leprechaun gold is reputed to be. However, as you will see further on, the association between the Pentacles/Earth energies continues. Our prosperity springs from the land, the Earth, but is spread by the people, the Cauldron. It is the effort of the elves who turn the potential abundance of the land into prosperity for the people. These are not strictly delineated categories, but interwoven and overlapping energies. We may look at them separately to understand them, but in truth they are One.

We could say that the direction of these realms of Faerie depend upon one's position on the Earth, in the same way that the devote Muslim turns toward Mecca to pray and whether he turns east or west, north or south depends on where he is in relationship to Mecca. But where is our Mecca, where is our Faerie? It is, in a sense, always within us. It is not a specific place upon the Earth but a dimension to which we connect within ours'elves. Some might propose that Faerie portals exist at specific spots, wild spaces, sacred centers, or ley line convergences (as in Freda Warrington's great novel *Elfland*), and if one wishes to orient ones'elf to a specific outer spot as a threshold to Faerie one may certainly do so. But again we say to you, the Way to Elfin is within, and viewing the passage into Elfin as we would view a journey in the material realm where we go north or east, etc., while similar, is not quite accurate.

Therefore these elves have un-attached the realm of Elfin from the four directions. Rather than think of them as North, East, South and West, we suggest they are outer circles, as those that ripple from a stone thrown into a pond (the Sacred Pool) and moving outward. They are not directions, but dimension of space that surround, even clothe the center of our being/spirit, our magic circle, and our eald. Ovyryn represents the material world that surrounds us. It is the world into which we strive to manifest Faerie and the Magic.

Avalan, is the realm of feelings, and is strongly interpenetrated with Ovyryn because feelings are so closely associated with sensation, the province of the physical body. Intyrnalys is the dimension of air, or mental energy, and interacts with the dimensions of Ovyryn easily, creating emotions. Uvynde is the realm of fire, or energy and will power. When we direct our will into the planes of energetic awareness, we can guide our aroused emotions, and move the material world with our magic. These realms don't exist simply in four different directions but are Within us, and our magic circle, and Beyond us. Through them we can move and affect the world.

In an elfin circle, instead of summoning or arousing the four directions, we awaken the four primary dimensions (there are more than four dimensions, but we need not go into those higher realms here, and all of these higher realms are accessed through our center, Elfynea). They surround our circle and can be summoned by turning in a circle as one calls to them, or from any of the four directions as the elf wills. This understanding of the magic will be effective whether one is in the Northern Hemisphere or the Southern, whether on the Earth or out in Space.

CHAPTER 9:

THE FIVE DIMENSIONS

Most witches and magicians evoke the four directions, but we elves being a star people find the four directions as a less than adequate process of evocation and prefer instead to evoke the five dimensions of Elfin, as the following will reveal:

Uvynde: the Dimension of Energetic and Radiance Spirit and the Staff of Power

Uvynde is the dimension of fire and energetic spirit. It is ethereal in nature and like flame is physical and yet not solid. It is related to the aspect of illumination and radiance. Its treasure is the Spear of Victory, which we've previously shown is related to the Spear of Destiny, or Spear of Longinus that pierced the side of Jesus, as well as the Spear of Genghis Khan. It brings victory to those who possess it. However, how is that different, and how do we distinguish it as being the power of victory, from the Sword of Nuada (another tool of war), which cannot be escaped. The sword is a weapon of discrimination, of the truth. It is hand held and, except in rare cases of desperation where it is thrown, it is always wielded by the warrior's hand. This indicates to us that the power of truth and discrimination must always begin with our own s'elves.

The Spear of Lugh, in contrast, grants victory to those who hold it, but it is also, like the arrow, a projectile, thus giving it the meaning of extension in space over distances, thus it is a symbol of communication, particularly of issuing orders or directives, that is communicating one's will. It is in this form that it becomes the wizard's staff, and the magician's wand, and denotes the power to affect events at a distance. The spear/staff/wand extends our reach and our realm. It is a symbol of expansion and is extraverted in nature, whereas for these elves, at least, the sword is an introverted symbol of defense, for we are ever safe in the truth.

In evoking Uvynde and the power of the Spear/Staff, we call forth success and victory in our creative projects and the expansion of our magic circle. We increase our power by increasing our powers, that is to say by developing our own true s'elves. However, because its power comes when one holds it, it makes us aware that the greatest power a ruler has, is their own example, which means applying the rules first and foremost to their own s'elf. The regents of Elfin are not the exception to the rules, they are the rule, they are the shining example of wisdom, fairness, and higher, which is to say, more evolved being. Their lives are the models that serve to guide and inspire our lives.

While the spear connects, reaches out, such expansion, even when done with the best intentions and in the most loving and kind ways, as is the Way of the Elfin, seldom goes unchallenged for long, which will bring us inevitably to Intyrnalys the realm of the sword of truth, from which, no one can escape.

If you choose to evoke these dimensions using the four directions, then Uvynde is the direction of the south and can be evoked by enchanting:

MIGHTY SPIRIT OF THE SOUTH

FILL US WITH YOUR FIRE

THAT WE SHALL OUR WILL EVER PURSUE

TO FILL OUR TRUE DESIRE

AND ENERGIZED WE'LL EVER BE

AND ON OUR PATH NEVER TIRE

TILL WE DO ELFIN BRING AGAIN

AND FAERIE WE DO SIRE

Or if you are evoking the Dimensions enchant:

UVYNDE, GREAT AND WONDROUS

FILLED WITH RADIANT LIGHT

ILLUMINATE OUR SPIRITS

AND GUIDE US THROUGH THE NIGHT

AND LEAD US TO THAT RADIANT LAND

WE'VE SEEN WITH VISION'S SIGHT

WHERE EACH ACCORDED HIR JUST DUE

KNOWS HIR SPIRIT BRIGHT

Intyrnalys: the Dimension of Air/Gas, the Mental Plane, and the Sword of Truth

As we've said these elves associate Gorias, one of the five sacred cities of the Sidhe, to Intyrnalys, the realm of the mind and to the Sword of Nuada, one of the four magical treasures of the Ancient Elfin. If you wish to use the four directions, Gorias is related to the East.

The great Elfin Sage Tymlere tells us that the West is the direction of the future, the ever-ongoing fulfillment of the vision and potential of the Elfin people, both individually and collectively. That vision is born in, and that potential derived from, the East, the Ancestors, the Past. The west is the direction in which, for the most part, the pioneering members of humanity have moved in order to establish new societies and thus the farther west one goes, or so the Sage tells us, the more likely one is to encounter more advanced and open minded people. Our own experience is that, like the dimensional nature of the elfin realms that surround us, open-minded people, which to us most often means elves, can be found here and there all over the globe. It may be true that there are more elves in one area than another at this time, but that is only a temporary happenstance.

For on a globe and on the spiral of evolution, one cannot go west without eventually arriving in the East from whence one came, for the west is connected in a complimentary fashion to the east, as we are connected, no matter how much we've grown and changed, to our childhood and our ancestors. Therefore, when elves speak of our Ancient Future, we are speaking of the realization in actuality of the vision that has always existed in potential within us. The past and the future exist within us in the ever transforming Now.

For calling this power as a direction, turn to the east and raised the Athame or sword and enchant:

SACRED SPIRITS OF THE EAST

WHOSE VISION TRUE DOTH NEVER CEASE

DO BRING FORTH IN OUR VERY LIVES

AND SHED ON US YOUR POWERS WISE

THAT ELFIN WE MAY REALIZE.

Legend holds that no enemy can escape the Sword of Nuada. The sword has traditionally been associated with the masculine in contrast to the chalice, which represents the feminine. Thus, for many Wiccans, plunging the Athame into the chalice is a symbolic enactment of sexual congress, a union of the masculine and feminine. While the sword, like the masculine, is often seen as an aggressive energy, these elves have always seen the sword as a defensive tool, which strikes only to protect. In that way, it is paired with the shield. We have an ancient saying among us that Love is our shield and Truth our sword. For surely Truth, by which we mean not a group of opinions or ideas, but the true nature of reality, is the sword that no one can escape.

But again, we suggest that the Sword of Nuada, which is also Excalibur, is a later assignation of this treasure. It is said that we should turn our swords into ploughshares, but in truth it was plowshares that were turned into swords. The Age of the Warrior cults, the conquering Horse Lords, was preceded by the Age of Agriculture, where the great treasure was a plough. Prior to that we were hunter-gatherers and our treasure was not a plough, but what? We suggest the bow and arrow. Thus the true treasure of Intyrnalys is the magical bow and arrow. It is Elf-shot, the magical and invisible arrows of the fae used, as legends tells us, by our ancestors. Although, we could also associate the bow and arrow with the spear of Lugh, and the elf dart, the blow dart with this power since it is propelled by air. At the same time, the blow dart/elf dart is blown though a hollow tube and this tube would be the wizard's staff, which is another form of the spear as we've noted previously. You be the judge as to where the magical Elf Dart that flies unseen and never misses should be placed, with the realms of fire, Uvynde, or of air, Intyrnalys. But clearly, Elf Shot, the magic arrow or dart, is one of our secret magical treasures.

This leads us, however, to a central and vital question. Who truly are our ancestors? If you ask that of most folks you will be immediately told of their parents, etc. as we've previously noted. And surely, we cannot deny that our bodies are descended from the genetic contributions of our parents. But what of our minds, our spirits and our souls? Have they not ancestors as well? Many Wiccans, Pagans and Elfinkind, of which these elves are all three, have genetic parents and grandparents, etc. who, not only do not share our views on spirituality and religion, but who may even ridicule or be hostile to those views. And while these elves, honor these folks, none-the-less, for having contributed to our being, we note that often our ancestors of spirit, soul and mind are to be found Elsewhere.

It is these beings, the ones who nurtured our souls with love, who enlightened our minds, who awakened us to our true natures that we honor, as well as our genetic ancestors, when we turn to the East or evoke the dimension of Intyrnalys. Those who taught us magic, those who inspired us with their wisdom, those who saw a potential in us that no others saw at the time, those who nurtured us instead of putting us down, all those are our true ancestors, and to them we give our thanks by turning to the future and nurturing others who are now searching as once we searched, who hunger in their soul as once we hungered, whose spirits cry out for encouragement, sometimes, just to get through another day. For the greatest thanks we can give them is to keep the Vision that they shared with us alive, by passing it on.

BLESSED ELFIN SPIRITS OF THE PAST
YOU ARE NOT FORGOTTEN
IN US, YOU LIVE ETERNALLY
AND IN THOSE WE HAVE BEGOTTEN
TILL ONCE AGAIN THE CIRCLE TURNS
AND BORN ANEW YOU FIND
YOU'RE HEIR TO ALL YOUR MAGICS DONE
OF SPIRIT, SOUL AND MIND.

Avalan: the Dimension of Liquid/Water, the Realm of Feelings, the Magic Cauldron

Avalan is the dimension of the feelings, which as we've said are connected to the gross physical plane, or the body through sensations, the senses, and connected to the spiritual planes of being through the soulful nature. It is usually the soulful nature that arouses the feelings when one hears the Call of Elfin.

If you call the four directions Avalan would be associated with the West, the direction of the future. You will note that our connection to the future is through our feelings, or really our intuition. This is due to the fact that as we progress beyond the realms of mental development, which is the province or task of the 5th Root Race, we will develop our higher mental faculties that are intuitive in nature. This is an advanced evolution of the instinctual feelings that guided us before the development of the reasoning mind. This is not a rejection of the mind but a true evolution of mind power and an advance of the powers of the soul. Doubt will be replaced by greater certainty. It is not that we will give up questioning, for the Quest goes ever on. However, an inner surety will guide us and while we will surely question many things, our inner s'elves will not be among them. We will know ours'elves more truly and be more confident in ours'elves and our chosen direction.

If you call the directions, you may wish to use the following enchantment:

WE CALL THE SPIRITS OF THE WEST

THE REALM OF ALL THAT IS TO BE

WHERE WE KNOW OURS'ELVES AS TRULY ONE

AND WE LIVE EVER FREE

AND WITH YOUR GUIDANCE WE'LL BE GRACED

AND TRAVEL FARTHER ON
INTO THE REALMS OF FAERIE TRUE
AS WE BRING THE COMING DAWN

The ancient treasure associated with Avalan is the Cauldron. However, there is more than one form of this cauldron. There is the Cauldron that is a never-ending source of food and nourishment, similar to Jesus' dividing of the loaves and fishes. It is also seen in the form of the Leprechaun's Pot of Gold (relating it to the Earth/solid dimension) and the Witches' Cauldron. Also, it is related to the Cornucopia, or the Horn of Plenty (also associated with the Earth/Solid dimension of Ovyryn), and as a horn is thus related to the Horn of Gabriel or Gabriel's Trumpet that announces Judgment Day and the Rising of the Dead (thus relating it to the dimension of Air/Gas). We elves have a form of Gabriel's trumpet that we call the Horn of Summoning. It calls our people to us and no matter how far they are away all elfin hear its call. It is what calls us back to Faerie. Although it does not blow or trumpet so much as sings.

The Rising of the Dead brings us to the second major aspect of this magical cauldron, which is the Cauldron of Rebirth in which the wounded or dead could be placed and by doing so healed or reborn. (see: *Mabinogion*, translated by Lady Charlotte Guest). And as we've mentioned previously the Cauldron it is another form of the Mirror of Galadriel, which is related to the sacred pool at the heart of Elfin where all ills are healed. If one drinks the waters of this pool one is gifted with immortality. This is the Spring of Eternal Life, or the Fountain of Youth that Ponce de Leon went in search of (see the movies *The Fountain* with Hugh Jackman {although it is a bit slow} and *Tuck Everlasting*). As you can see all these dimensions and their treasures are interlinked, rather like the body, feelings, mind, soul, and spirit, which is in part why these elves prefer to think of them as dimensions rather than directions.

IF YOU WOULD SUMMON THE DIMENSION OF AVALAN, ENCHANT:

AVALAN, OH REALM OF LOVE

SHED YOUR BLESSINGS HERE

OPEN UP OUR EAGER HEARTS

WITH LOVE THAT IS SINCERE

AND GUIDE US TOWARD THAT MAGIC DAY

WHEN ALL SHALL BE AS ONE

WE'RE GATHERED DEEP IN ELVEN LAND

BENEATH THE TWILIGHT SUN

Ovyryn: the Dimension of Earth/Solid, The Stone of Fal

Ovyryn is the Dimension of the Earth/Solid/Material realm and thus involves all things having to do with the physical body, prosperity and manifestation on the material realm of our desires. When using directions, it is associated with the North. The Stone of Fal is usually said to be its magical treasure. This stone sings when the true king/regent sits upon it. It is thus also connected to the Stone of Scone of Scotland and all magical stones: stone circles, menhirs, and dolmens. The Stone of Scone is also called the Stone of Destiny (note the relation to the Spear of Destiny) and the Coronation stone. It is said that the King and the Land are One, that is to say mystically united, and these magical stones represent this idea.

Just a five-minute walk from where these elves live, there is on Waikiki Beach four shaman stones/boulders that were brought to Hawaii from Polynesia by the shamans of those islands for connecting the lands and bringing the power of healing to

Hawaii. These, too, are magical stones that would relate to the dimension of Ovyryn.

The magic stones, however, are also associated with gemstones and crystals, thus regents wear gems in their crowns and these gems are the visible symbol of the material wealth and prosperity that the true nobility bring to a realm.

These elves, however, also associate the Shield of Protection, the Shield of Love with this dimension, Ovyryn, indicating that our powers of enchantment and courtesy are every bit as important, perhaps even more so, in protecting our ealds (elven homes) as the stones, gems, and material wealth are. Note that the shield is also the Pantacle (magical Seal) of the Spirit, the Coin (thus relating the shield to prosperity), and the Magic Circle. The shield, of course, is paired with both the spear and the sword.

However, also note that gems and crystals fall under that domain of the air, since it is crystals that convey and pick up sound waves in radios. Crystals are used to transmit our thoughts over great distances. As we've said already, the treasures link the dimensions. They are like portals to various parts of one's realm. In that way, the Palantir, the Seeing Stones in Tolkien's novels, are also associated with these magical treasures and, in themselves, show how the treasures link the realms. They are, in effect, the crystal ball commonly associated with fortune telling, only functioning more like a modern cell phone.

If you call directions, you may wish to use the following summoning as an example:

HEAR US, SPIRITS OF THE NORTH

AWAKEN TO OUR VOICE

AND HASTEN HENCE AND LEND YOUR AID

BY YOUR LOVING CHOICE

THAT WE MAY WITH OUR POWERS MERGED
ACHIEVE A MAGIC GREAT
AND BRING FORTH THE VISION OF FAERIE BORN
FOR WHICH WE ALL AWAIT.

Or if you, like us, call the Dimensions, you may wish to
consider something similar to this enchantment:

OVYRYN, REALM OF GREAT SUCCESS
WHERE ALL OUR DREAMS COME TRUE
MADE REAL BY OUR PERSISTENT-NESS
IN EVERYTHING ACT WE DO
ELFIN COMES TO MANIFEST
WITHIN US AND FAR ROUND
MAKE REAL THE MAGICS WE ENCHANT
UPON THIS SACRED GROUND

Elfynea: the Dimension of the Inner S'elf, the Soulful Spirit Manifest, the Sacred Pool, The Rings of Power

Elfynea is at the center of our being. It is connected directly to
The Magic, the Source of All Being. Its direction is always
within, thus it symbolizes the magician within hir magic circle.
It is ever Centered, that is to say it is ever the Center. All things,
energies and dimensions swirl about it. The treasures associated
with it are the Sacred Pool of Healing and Immortality, and the
Rings of Power.

As we've shown the Sacred Pool of Healing and Immortality is connected with the Cauldron of Rebirth and the Mirror of Galadriel, thus in this was esoterically linked to all Magic Mirrors. The Rings of Power would be associated with the Three Rings of the Elves in Tolkien's stories. However, note that in his tales the rings are held and wielded by great beings, by Kings and Queen's of Elfin. The real ring of power, however, as these elves see it, is the Faerie Ring around which the elfin people dance to summon up the powers of the Earth, draw down the powers of the Moon, and clothe us in the radiance of the Stars. The power does not reside in one, or in several leaders, except as representatives of the Elven People. The true power arises from collective unity of the Elven people. The Faery Ring is the true ring of power and is thus associated with the Magic Circle. All other rings of power are merely symbols for that true ring of power, the Union, or extended family if you will, of the Elfin/Faerie peoples.

To evoke Elfynea, you may wish to chant:

FROM THIS CIRCLE BRIGHT AND TRUE
ARISE GREAT POWERS TO RENEW
OUR TROTH, OUR PEOPLE, AND OUR PLEDGE
TO REACH ACROSS THE THORNY HEDGE
AND THUS TO BUILD THE RAINBOW BRIDGE
AND SO THE WORLD TO WOO.

CHAPTER 10:

ABOVE AND BELOW

As we mentioned earlier if you are calling directions, you have north, south, east, west and the center of the circle, thus Without and Within; but how about up and down, or above and below. As we pointed out to you the Hermetic adage As Above, So Below, that is the macrocosm is reflected in and by the microcosm, is called As Within, So Without/or So Beyond among these elves, that is the world at large and the dimensions beyond reflect the magic of Faerie. They are responsive and interactive dimensions. There is a relationship between them.

However, we still commonly find the idea of above and below used in social and evolutionary terms. We speak of upper classes and lower classes. People climb higher and higher on the ladder of success. We think of evolving higher spiritually. This partially comes from the old idea that Heaven is above us, and Hell below. People speak of someone being very high spiritually. As well as the idea that people who are less evolved than we, are beneath us, even beneath our contempt.

As an idea, it has its place. It is natural to have a concept of evolving beyond where we were previously. However, two things occur to us. The first is that Seelie elves usually speak of getting deeper into Elfin or Faerie, that is more and more in touch with our true Elfin nature. We are not going up, that is to say getting higher, so much as going in, getting deeper into ours'elves and thus into Faerie. The second thing is that evolution to us is like a group of elves fording a high and swift moving stream. Some of the elves secure thems'elves to a tree or other stable position, and another elf holds on to them as sHe ventures toward the water, another takes her hand or arm and ventures farther, another climbs along this line and goes farther still until the line extends across the stream, until the elves who have crossed secure thems'elves to a tree or boulder on the other shore, and those that remained on the first side start climbing along the line to the far shore. Finally, the last person to climb up upon the far shore is the first elf to reach that shore. To the Seelie elves, this is ever the process and symbolic representation of spiritual evolution. Those who have gone farther are there to help those behind them to pass on. For us, spiritual evolution is like a game of leap frogging. If we are higher than our others, it only means we have the responsibility to reach down to them and help them to climb above us so they in turn will help us climb higher. The deeper we go into Elfin the more we call out to those who are near to help them find the way. If someone wants to know what the Elven Way is, it is this: we reach out to our kindred beneath us climbing the Trees of Life and help them come a bit farther.

However, if you use the directions below and above you may find the following incantations useful:

WE CALL OUT TO THOSE ABOVE US

TO GUIDE US ON THE WAY

AND SHOW TO US THE SECRET PATHS

THAT HELP ASPIRING FAE

AND WE IN TURN WILL REACH OUT, TOO

TO THOSE WHO COME BEHIND

SO THEY WILL WITH OUR ENCOURAGEMENT

THE WAY TO ELFIN FIND

And:

WE HEARING YOU CALLING IN YOUR HEART
AND WE ARE CALLING, TOO
AND LEAVING MAGIC SIGNS THAT WILL
THE WAY TO ELFIN SHEW
SO FINDING THEM YOU'LL SEE THE TRUTH
THAT WE ARE WITH YOU STILL
FOR MAGICS WE HAVE LEFT FOR YOU
YOUR VISIONS TO FULFILL

This book, dear kin, and the others we have written are the magic signs we've left for those searching for Elfin/Faerie in and beyond the world. We bless you and grant your true wishes.

CHAPTER 11:

A WORD ABOUT TRUE WISHES

What is a True Wish? Or what is one's True Will, as opposed to some other form of will? One can wish for many things but not all those things are true wishes. What distinguishes a true wish from a common wish are a few very simply things.

A true wish always furthers the individual toward the perfection of the individual elf's soulful nature and the perfection of one's being, that is to say one's body, mind, personality and spirit. Addictions cannot be true wishes. Obsessions sometimes can be, but seldom are. If the wish harms others or yours'elf, it is not a true wish. If it enslaves you, as addictions do, it is not a true wish. True wishes liberate, they enlighten, they uplift, they further our nature in their fulfillment, because everyone deep within hir own s'elf wishes to be more perfect, better, more powerful, and more at ease with hir own s'elf. A true wish sets us free, it empowers us, it helps us to be more of who we truly are, who we are destined, by our natures, to be.

"May all your True Wishes come to be" is a different spell than "May all your wishes come true" as faerie tales often demonstrate when a person has hir wish granted only to be undone by hir own greed and lack of spiritual development.

MAY ALL YOUR TRUE WISHES COME TO BE.

Part Three:
The Laws of Magic of the Seelie Elves

CHAPTER 12:

SEELIE ELF LAWS OF

KARMIC DYNAMICS

We Seelie Elves view Karma as Luck. What you do either brings you good luck/karma or bad luck/karma. It's as simple as that.

1. IN THE END, EVERYONE GETS EXACTLY WHAT SHE DESERVES. IN THE MEANTIME, YOU MAY HAVE TO PUT UP WITH A LOT OF CRAZINESS. AND NOT GOOD CRAZINESS, WHICH IS TO SAY ELF CRAZINESS, BUT MEAN AND CRUEL HUMAN CRAZINESS, AND SOME TIMES VIOLENT INHUMAN CRAZINESS, BUT IN THE END, IT ALL BALANCES OUT.

2. ON THE WAY, EVERYONE GETS A LOT OF WHAT THEY DON'T DESERVE, BOTH FORTUNATE AND UNFORTUNATE. OUR MAGIC IS NOT THE ONLY MAGIC IN THE UNIVERSE, AND OFTEN NOT THE MOST POWERFUL MAGICS, EITHER. ALL WE CAN DO IS TAKE RESPONSIBILITY FOR OUR OWN MAGICS, AND HAVE FAITH IN THE SYSTEM, WHICH IS TO SAY, THE DIVINE MAGIC FROM WHICH WE ALL ORIGINATE.

3. ULTIMATELY, WHAT YOU DO WITH WHAT YOU GET, BOTH DESERVED AND UNDESERVED, DETERMINES WHAT YOU DO DESERVE AND GET. WE EVER LIVE IN THE HERE AND NOW, YET WE ARE ALWAYS IN THIS FOR THE LONG HAUL, AND WE EVER REMEMBER OUR ANCESTORS.

CHAPTER 13:

DOOM, FATE, GEAS, KARMA,

DHARMA, AND DESTINY

Doom is a word that comes from Anglo-Saxon and means Judgment or Law. In modern times we tend to use it to mean the apocalypse is fast upon us, but in ages past it often mean a directive compelling one to carry out a particular act or deed. In the Lord of the Rings it is used much in the way that the word Fate is used. So we may say that we elves living in this current era are doomed, or fated, to put up with a various cultures that do not believe we exist, and that ridicule our culture without ever even bothering to try to understand, or even asking, what we mean when we say we are elves, and our reasons for doing so.

Geas is usually found in fantasy novels and indicates a spell or a curse placed upon someone to force them to carry out a quest or other directive. In that way it is like the word doom, however it has it further addition of a magical compulsion. The Geas that is upon most elves is the one we placed upon ours'elves when we swore to incarnate into this world and inspirit it with Elfin/Faerie magic, to awaken our kindred, and to help guide them back home. Which is to say to the center of their own beings where they will find their true s'elves, and thus their most intimate connection to Elfin. And we have sworn to carry out this task despite the popular notions of the world that ridicule us, the numerous distractions of the world both positive and negative, both pleasurable and painful that draw our people's attention and consciousness in a never-ending attempt to ensnare them in the tangled threads and designs of those who seek to control us and wish to keep us from knowing the depth and power of the elfin soul.

Karma is usually used to mean the results in one's current life from one's acts in a previous life. This has a rather simple cause and effect aspect to it, but it also has more subtle aspects, the results of our thoughts and intentions. As we've said many times in these books, we create our world in all we do. However, karma also has the aspect that associates it with fate. How do we answer the question why bad things happen to good people? Our karma is not only a function of our actions, good or bad, but also a result of the world we have incarnated within. It is also a reflection, not only of what we have done, what we have failed to do, but also what we are currently unable to do. We die because we have not yet mastered the material world. That is our fate, that is our karma, but it is also our dharma.

Dharma is the quest we have voluntarily undertaken. We have in many ways chosen to incarnate now, which is when and where we are needed, and do what we can to uplift our people. This choice to incarnate now also creates a fate for us, for we are fated to deal with the circumstances of this dimension, this world, and its current level of evolutionary development. This means that some times bad things may happen, happenstance, and this is our fate and our karma. But the Universe always balances out. All we endure that we did not create ours'elves will be balanced out in positive benefits later. This is just wishful thinking? Well, yes it is wishful thinking, but not just wishful thinking. We're faerie folk. It is our power and our job description to grant wishes.

Is there such a thing as Destiny? Yes, but it is seldom as the world tends to see it, in terms of so and so is destined to be king, and so on. Each person, every soulful spirit has a destiny to know and become its true s'elf, to perfect its'elf endlessly becoming ever more, ever greater, ever growing, ever developing and evolving as a being, and in this way to realize its Divine, by which we mean, Magical/Miraculous Nature.

Know this, beloved kindred, no matter what you encounter in this life, what difficulties, obstacles or obstructions, what suffering you endure, the magic of Elfin/Faerie is always reaching out to you. It doesn't matter if you are lost, get lost, or forget who you are, we will find you eventually. Still, it is you who has to find your way home, and so we have instilled the world with magic, with radiant signs, omens, and guideposts to indicate the way. We have left bits of magic all about. We have released hints to seek you. We have spread stardust to the far corners of the Earth, and we are forever calling your true name to guide you home to us, for your kindred ever await you in Elfin. And all we ask of you, blessed one, is that you leave trinkets of magic and tokens of elvish love for those who will come after you.

Part Four:
The Magical
Community of
The Seelie Elves

CHAPTER 14:

STARTING YOUR OWN

SANCTUARY/TEMPLE/

GROVE/VORTEX

You can start your own group, sanctuary, temple, coven, grove, vortex, etc. of Seelie Elf Magic. The following pages give a general indication of what that association could be like, the levels of development, study and adeptship. However, it should be noted that while the grades of accomplishment are listed sequentially, few people actually study in that manner. Most elfin enchanters are working on several levels at the same time. Also, while we have indicated levels of attainment, the simple fact is that Nature=Life is the true Initiator. And further, that the more structured and formal your organization is, the more serious it is, the more dependent or insistent it is on having a strict hierarchy, the less you will attract true Seelie Elves. Seelie Elves are not impressed by titles and love to laugh at pompous asses. (Although we tend to do that in private unless they are particularly ostentatious with their pomposity. Then they may be gifted with one of our knowing smiles.) Our associations are ever on the wing and a formal and structured magical organization tends to go against the nature of the elves.

The Sanctuary of the Seelie Elves

If you wish to have a true Seelie Elf Sanctuary, take note of the guidelines, then let it develop on its own, according to the needs, abilities, desires, and interactions of the interested elves you attract. A Seelie Elf Sanctuary is always shaped by those who participate in it. After all, its real function is to elevate its members.

A Seelie Elf Sanctuary functions on consensus. Everyone must agree on the decisions being made. However, independent action is always encouraged. The true Seelie Elf adept is a master at empowering people and encouraging them to think for thems'elves, and to act on their own initiative. The goal of the Seelie Elf Sanctuary is to instill the elves involved with confidence, to help them become greater enchanters.

We caution you against making an exclusive group in which your members can belong only to your group and no others. The true Seelie Elf group is always open. Sincere individuals are free to join or leave as they please (although there may be inner mysteries that are only revealed in time to those who persevere), and they are encouraged to explore all their interests, and to be in as many other groups as their interests dictate or draw them. However, loyalty to the group and to its members is essential. A Seelie Elf vortex is a magical family.

Neither force nor coercion, neither structure, nor hierarchy, or titles hold the Seelie Elf group together; rather it is a union bound by mutual attraction, common goals, shared will, and a love of the fun and excitement that always comes when elves gather. If the experience they have together is powerful and meaningful, it will resonate their entire lives. Having come together in the magic, we are forever connected. If that coming together is a positive one, which it nearly always is with the Seelie Elves, it will produce positive feelings and memories through time that will continue to fulfill and support our magic. In coming together to do our magic, no matter how brief the time, we are investing in our future, and dividends from that magic will come to us periodically through our lives bringing us blessings of starlight, moonlight, and wonders divine.

The most adept Seelie Elves are the most eager learners. They seldom resort to titles, but rather depend upon the power of their living aura to influence others. In general, however, Seelie Elves tend to relate to everyone on an equal basis. If a person is a novice and a beginner, then the elf is also an eager and open student. If someone claims sHe is the High Priest of So and So, or the Master of Such and Such, the elf gives hirs'elf an equally impressive title. This, of course, is merely a trick, and we in no way take our own titles, nor anyone else's, seriously. Our intention is always to relate to everyone as another aspirant upon the path of knowledge, wisdom, and s'elf fulfillment, which is the inner truth of all our relationships.

The Order of the Temple

Again, we remind you that elves are not inclined toward hierarchies, or even organizations for the most part. We ever prefer to think of ours'elves as families and tribes, packs, mobs, and bands. Yet, and this is particularly true for young elves and the newly awakened, there are elves who desire a bit of structure until they can feel secure enough, and confident enough, to be fully thems'elves among their others. Until one has a sense of who one truly is, it is hard to decide what direction to proceed in magically. Therefore, the following guideline is offered merely as a possibility for those who would gather a group of elves about in them in a vortex, or magical lodge, or what has been traditionally called a Rath or elf fort, a fortress of magic.

And remember, this is not intended as a step-by-step development, in which one becomes a Magician and then an Exorcist, and then graduates to Shaman, and so on. In our experience elves, once they have a true sense of their s'elves, tend to gravitate to particular forms of magic. Some feel an inclination toward being Sorcerers, others to being Wizards, from the very beginning. Many others simply blend them together into a Wizardly Sorcerous Conjuror, or something of that nature. The fact is, we elves, in studying something, tend to study it all.

Still, in studying magic we would suggest that the elf starts with the principles of White Magic and the ways of the Magician, learn Black Magic and the means of warding off negative influences, move on to Green Magic and the Principles of Healing and so on. This is not to say that one won't at the same time be studying and practicing, really doing Necromancy, that is to say honoring the traditions and the ancestors, and using the Oracles to connect with them and receive their guidance. In reality, elves tend to immediately begin studying their chosen field, or fields, while developing the underpinnings of the basic, intermediate and eventually advanced levels of magic. It is only natural that people should follow their own interests, and it is wise for the adept teacher to understand and use those interests in educating them. This, in truth, is the basis for all elven education.

And, in our experience elves don't often do this in a hierarchal sequential fashion, even though that is how we have, by necessity of the printed word, presented them here. We would suggest to the teacher/initiator of the vortex/rath that unless the aspirant is totally clueless, and sometimes even then, it is best to discover what hir interests are and to apply all lessons concerning magic to those interests as well as to hir current desires, circumstances and goals in the worlds, both mundane and imaginal. Thus if the aspirant is lonely, one offers hir spells of the Ganconer. If sHe is having financial difficulties, sHe is instructed in Conjuration and so on. And if sHe is like most people, many of these things will be going on at the same time. By attaching the lessons to the elf's life the lessons become vibrant and alive.

This is not to say that the basics of White and Black magic should be ignored, but that those lessons can best be incorporated into lessons on how to attract one's soul mate, while protecting one from predators or those who are simply not right for one. Basically, we give guidance according to the needs of those who come to us. We do not have a one size fits all magic. Traditionally, we elves have often been portrayed as tailors. And there is truth to this. We fit our magic to suit the individual elf who approaches us. Even if we have a class of a dozen or more individuals, we will still help each who approaches us to apply the lessons to the needs of hir life. It makes the magic come alive for them. The greatest transmissions are not of facts, spells and techniques of magick, but of the living vibration of elven magick.

Still, this is your vortex, and these are only suggestions. If you are an elf, you will do what you think is best no matter what we say, and that's exactly as it should be.

The following is shows a progress through elfin magical education as it would be seen in accordance to many traditional magical lodges:

PROBATIONER = MAGICIAN, WHITE MAGIC

NEOPHYTE = EXORCIST, BLACK MAGIC

ZEALOTOR = SHAMAN/HEALER, GREEN MAGIC

PRACTICUS = CONJUROR, ORANGE MAGIC

PHILOSOPHUS = SORCERER, PURPLE MAGIC

ADEPTUS MINOR = GANCONER, RED MAGIC

ADEPTUS MAJOR = WIZARD, BLUE MAGIC

ADEPTUS PERFECTUS = WARLOCK, YELLOW MAGIC

MAGISTER TEMPLI = NECROMANCER, GOLD MAGIC

MAGUS = THAUMATURGE, SILVER MAGIC

MAGUS SINGULARUS = ENCHANTER SUPREME (THE INVISIBLE MAN), RAINBOW MAGIC

Finally, we Seelie Elves assume all people are potential magicians. Some show much more potential than others, who are lifetimes, if not nearly forever it seems, away from this possibility, although, usually the difference is not ability but inclination. While we do not seek to convert anyone (a truly hopeless exercise), we always try to treat everyone as a potential friend, comrade, ally and accomplice, and are ever looking for those signs (such as intelligence, independence, and a sense of humor) that designate the practitioner of elfin magic.

Magician

It is expected that the Magician will make preliminary explorations into the occult subjects of hir choice. Newly awakened elfin magicians are often very hesitant and sensitive, and it is very important for the higher adepts to be gentle with the Magician Probationers, to go slowly, and let them progress at their own rate and urging. Most of all, the magician needs constant reinforcement, and encouragement.

This level is about reassurance and the development of confidence. Often, particularly at this stage, the individual is confronted by the taunting demons that challenge one's right to think and act for ones'elf, that make fun of one for thinking ones'elf an elf, and ridicule magic and one's association with it. The elfin magician needs to be reassured that this is truly a viable path, and most of all sHe needs true examples, living examples, of elfin magic. If you can make the magic come alive for someone, you've performed a great feat of magic; cast a spell that will transform hir life.

However, this cannot be faked. No unearned titles are a substitute for bringing the magic alive. In fact, no earned titles will do it either. Curiously, not even intention alone will perform this magic trick. However, if one lives one's life in the magic, surrounds ones'elf with Elfin, one need only do what they would do anyway and the aura of Elfin will surround one.

Nothing special is needed. Those who are ready will see/feel the magic, and those who are not will fade back into the world, perhaps to wander into Elfin at another time.

It is the duty of the Magician to arrive at an eclectic view, and to stop depending absolutely on the word of authority, to take what sHe wants from the books sHe studies and transform it to hir own needs. The Magician must make peace with hir parents or other figures of authority, and stop blaming them for whatever has gone wrong in hir life. SHe must also free hirs'elf from all prejudices concerning race, gender, religion, political belief, nationality, social status and wealth, or lack thereof, and understand that it is the magician and only the magician who has true power to alter the course of hir destiny. It doesn't matter who's to blame, the only question is what is sHe going to do about it. Accepting responsibility for one's life and magic is the first step to doing real magic and creating genuine changes in one's life and in one's world. Remember magic is about creating change by the power of one's Will guided by one's Intention.

Suggested Reading:

The Harry Potter Series
The Magicians and the Magician King by Lev Grossman

Suggested Viewing:

Simon: King of the Witches, starring Andrew Prine
The Harry Potter Movies

Exorcist

It is the work of the Exorcist to learn to defend hirs'elf on the astral plane. Also, sHe is advised to give up addictions, and other habits of thought and action that inhibit the fulfillment of hir will. Addictions are demons that control one. The Exorcist must learn to choose hir friends and acquaintances carefully, letting go of those relationships that lead one away from one's true path, and that keep one bound to the negative habits and outdated thought modes.

Thought modes, that is to say habitual ways of thinking, are often Introjects, or ideas that were instilled in one very early in life before one had much in the way of psychic s'elf defense. Often these demons speak in one's mind using the voice of the person who first instilled the Introject, usually one's parent or guardian. In as much as these admonitions, criticisms, and opinions interfere with one's magic and life, one needs to root them out. They are demons. However, in as much as they are harmless, it is often better just to tolerate them, or ignore them. In many ways the same is true of demons. If one struggles with them they grow stronger and waste one's time, interfering with one's magic and the fulfillment of one's will, which is, after all, their goal. By giving them no energy, by focusing the mind elsewhere as soon as one recognizes their voice, or the thought habit, they begin to starve. (See Object Relations Psychology for more on Introjections.)

Besides psychic s'elf defense, the Exorcist often begins the study of some form of martial arts, a study that may continue indefinitely. The Exorcist begins practicing techniques to induce out of the body experience, conscious or lucid dreaming, and astral travel.

It is the duty of the Exorcist to look after and protect the Magician Aspirants from the fears, terrors, and paranoia of the lower astral planes and the first confrontation they often experience between the true magic and their enculturated fears, and introjections, concerning it.

Remember, many aspirants have dabbled in the magical arts previously with some small success, which none-the-less frightened them because of the demon introjects that they carried in their psyche and ignored. They ignored them usually because of a current supposedly scientific prejudice that told them there is nothing to magic. Thus they ignored the early parental or religious introjections that told them not to dabble. When their magic actually produced results, and usually this comes because they functioned in a group, which thus created more power, those early warnings kicked in and the admonitions not to dabble came to the fore and they scared thems'elves, so reentry into the world of magic is doubly frightening for them.

Life, of course, can be dangerous. This is true if one is doing magic or driving down the street. But for those who have the courage to pursue magic despite their fears, the venture into Elfin can be glorious. It helps if the aspirant has a bit of wisdom, or in this case proper guidance so one does one's magic with precautions, and a true understanding of karma, which is the principle that everything we do returns to us. To understand this is to comprehend magic.

Suggested Readings:

The Black Magic Novels of Dennis Wheatley
(note that while we love these novels, Dennis Wheatley wrote from a cultural period where racial and cultural prejudice were commonly accepted and this should be understood as one reads his works.)
The Ninja Books by Stephen K. Hayes
The Ninja Books by Ashida Kim
Journey Out of the Body by Robert Monroe
Monkey and the White Boned Demon by Jill Morris
Magic Without Tears by Aleister Crowley
Principia Discordia or How I Found the Goddess and What I Did to Her When I Found Her.

Suggested Viewing:

Dark Forces, starring Robert Powell
The Last Wave, directed by Peter Weir, and starring Richard Chamberlain
Dreamscape, starring Dennis Quaid
Inception starring Leonardo DiCaprio

Shaman/Healer/Curandero

It is the work of the Shaman/Healer/Curandero to become in control of hir own body, both internal and external, through the study and practice of hatha yoga, meditation, and proper diet. To be a healer, one must be whole within one's own s'elf. There is a reason that elves are typically viewed as being svelte. This is does mean that one cannot be an elf if one is heavy set, but it is difficult to be a healer if one is not healthy and living a healthy lifestyle. The proverb found in Luke 4:23 of Physician, Heal Thys'elf, among the elves would be Tymothy 4:20 Healer, Live Healthy.

The Shaman Healer must obtain a positive outlook on all aspects of hir life, and needs to overcome and conquer any tendencies toward depression and negative thinking. She is advised to learn and practice the art of Positive Thinking and Imagination. There are many books on Positive Thinking and the power thereof, but it is also important that our daydreams and fantasies be healthy as well, for these come from and connect to our right, spatial brain, and link us to our dreams, our unconscious s'elves, and thus to the psyches of all others. The Elfin Healer masters positive thinking, positive visualization and positive imagination.

The Shaman Healer learns to become careful in everything sHe says, so sHe's has a positive and healing influence on others. The Shaman Healer learns to affect people's subconscious through suggestion and will power, and to accept responsibility for doing so. And this is a huge responsibility and it is vital that one does this with proper Intention of helping and healing. This must be a selfless act, truly done for the benefit of the other.

It behooves the Healer to study hypnotherapy, massage, herbalism, chiropractic, acupuncture, nutrition, Reiki and other healing arts, and to become proficient in one or more of these. The main systems of divination for the Shaman/Healer often involve iridology, foot reflexology, and other arts that read the condition of the body.

It is the duty of the Healer within the Vortex/Sanctuary to help keep the Exorcists from taking their work too seriously, and to remind them that a sense of humor is one of the most effective weapons in our arsenal against those who have erroneously chosen to interfere with our magics, and to always approach their work with the future in mind, that is with an eye to healing and to evolution.

Suggested Reading:

Healing Stoned by Julia Lorusso and Joel Glick
The Way of the Shaman by Michael Horner
Cosmic Serpent by Jeremy Narby
Angel Tech: A Modern Shaman's Guide to Reality Selection by Antonio Alli

Suggested Viewing:

Resurrection starring Ellen Burstyn
Housekeeping starring Christine Lahti

Conjuror

The Conjuror needs to begin the daily use of the I Ching. It is the task of the Conjuror to secure hir material existence, and in particular, set about finding hir true, proper, and fulfilling work, which is both financially lucrative, and creatively and emotionally satisfying. The I Ching will serve are a guide to help one navigate through the material world using hir magic. One might use the tarot, however the I Ching is more of an outer voice than the tarot, and less likely to be interpreted according to the whims and desires, prejudices and particularly preconceptions of the Conjuror. It stands outside the Conjuror and speaks to hir as an independent voice. And having begun this practice the wise conjuror continues consulting its advice ever after. (See our book *The Elven Book of Changes: a Magical Interpretation of the I Ching*, which is particularly written for elfin folk and magic users of all sorts.)

The Conjuror must proceed to do whatever is necessary to further hir education and job skills. SHe must strive toward becoming financially independent ... to be hir own boss, and even when sHe works for others sHe should always consider hirs'elf as an independent contractor. The goal here, however, is for hir to pursue hir own creative endeavors and to make them financially viable for hir. Ultimately, sHe needs to do what sHe loves doing and support hirs'elf by doing it.

It behooves the Conjuror to study the Qabalah, and the Tree of Life, and to comprehend the integrated nature of economics, as well as the profitability of coordinated effort, the principles of success through planning, and step-by-step progress. This is not to say that the Tree of Life is principally about economics. The Tree of Life covers and concerns the all of Life, but by understanding Life in its greater manifestations, we come to understand how to conjure its principles on the material plane and create success there. (You may wish to check out our book *The Elven Tree of Life Eternal: the Quest for the True S'Elf.*)

The Conjuror is directed to learn not only the power of accumulation, but just as importantly, the powers of generosity and distribution. It is common practice for the Conjuror to give to street beggars and other needy folk, for these folks are usually on the edge of life and therefore quite often closer, that is to say more attuned, to the world of the spirits, although not always, perhaps even seldom, in what most folks would think of as a spiritual fashion. They are often closer to the wild spirits than the tamer beings that hang out near churches, although since many churches help the homeless, they have their own connection to these wild spirits.

The Conjuror is responsible for watching over the Shaman Healer and making sure hir positive thinking heals all attitude is grounded in practical reality. That is to say that hir positive thinking is not mere wishful thinking, but reflects reality in a positive form, otherwise there is a tendency to ignore and repress feelings about problems and conflicts, and that isn't at all a healthy thing to do.

Suggested Reading:

Magic in Theory and Practice by Aleister Crowley
Magic Without Tears by Aleister Crowley
The Tree of Life by Israel Regardie
The Seven Laws of Money by Michael Phillips
How to Start Your Own Country by Erwin S. Strauss
Do What You Love; The Money Will Follow by Marsha Sinetar
The Seven Spiritual Laws of Success: A Pocketbook Guide to Fulfilling Your Dreams by Deepak Chopra

Suggested Viewing:

Brimstone and Treacle starring Sting
Dirty Rotten Scoundrels starring Michael Caine and Steve Martin
Or: Bedtime Story starring David Niven and Marlon Brando
The Riches starring Minnie Driver and Eddie Izzard
Revolver directed by Guy Richie

Sorcerer

The Sorcerer is advised to keep a daily journal, which is often called the Book of Shadows, of hir magic works and experiences. The Sorcerer endeavors to attain direct mystical contact with Nature, and thereby hir own nature, and to develop hir own style in all that sHe does.

It is the task of the Sorcerer to strive toward creating a masterpiece, a major work, or body of work in hir chosen area of creativity: to write a book, make a video, a movie, a gallery of paintings, hir own tarot deck, or whatever contribution to art, creativity, magic and hir culture that most appeals to hir.

The Sorcerer is particularly in a position to create tools of magic, such as wands, staffs, pantacles (seals), or magical raiment, and to create works of art or craft that will enhance the magical atmosphere and beauty of the Sanctuary and its furnishings. The Sorcerer is tasked with making the Sanctuary better, more beautiful, more magical, especially enhancing its ambience, vibration, and atmosphere. The Sanctuary should hum, ring, vibrate, radiate with magic.

The true Sorcerer aids the Conjurors to understand the artistic and spiritual aspects of making and investing money. This means using money to create art, but also seeing the process of moneymaking and pecuniary activities as a creative, artistic endeavor. The Sorcerer also accepts the responsibility to encourage all others in the Vortex to strive to do their best in everything they do. To make all their acts works of art. To make their life truly one of style, giving the phrase Life Style true meaning. In a sense, one might say that it is the Sorcerer's task to help hir others give meaning to their style and style to their meaning. To the Elven mind, these aspects of being and culture are intimately related; our culture arises from our Beingness.

Suggested Readings:

The Don Juan Series by Carlos Castaneda
The Secrets of Dr. Taverner by Dion Fortune
Drawing on the Right Side of the Brain by Betty Edwards
The Abolition of Work by Bob Black
Human History Viewed as Sovereign Individuals versus Manipulated Masses by Valorian Society
Visualization: Directing the Movies of Your Mind by Adelaide Bry
Lateral Thinking: Creativity Step by Step by Edward de Rono

Suggested Viewing:

Onmyogi 1 and 2, starring Mansai Nomura

Ganconer (Love Talker – Love Whisperer)

The Ganconer is directed to create an aura of beauty and sexuality about hirs'elf. The Ganconer endeavors to make hirs'elf as attractive as possible on all planes of being: physical, mental, spiritual, and emotional. The Ganconer transforms hir personality into one that is magnetic and exciting, and learns to deal effectively and confidently in all hir personal communications. The Ganconer is aware that romance and sexual energy underlies and influences nearly all relationships, including business relationships, and nearly all other interactions.

The Ganconer devotes hirs'elf to the study of Tantric Yoga and the principles of Sex Magic. The Ganconer studies the power of body language and learns to use it at will. People are not only attracted to the Ganconer; they just like hir. There is just something about the Ganconer, something magical, something special. SHe just makes you want to smile, and you always feel good about yours'elf after interacting with hir. SHe does not need to seduce, however, for people come to hir willingly. Hir effort is almost entirely directed toward the others sHe encounters.

Matchmaking is another aspect for study by the Ganconer, who is directed not only to find hir own personal mates and lovers but learns how to bring others together in combinations that create energy and excitement. SHe understands which individuals will get along well with each other, and brings together those who are romantically and creativity well matched. In all that sHe does, sHe furthers others on their path.

It is the duty of the Ganconer to watch over the Sorcerers in particular, introducing them to people and events that are inspirational to their creative development; but the Ganconer also helps all the members of the Vortex/Sanctuary, giving them hints about how they may improve thems'elves and thus their success in relationship.

Suggested Reading:

Sexual Secrets by Nik Douglas and Penny Slinger
Genitology: reading the genitals by Dr. Seymore Klitz and Dr. Ima
Peeper (an amusing tongue in cheek book for Diviners)
The Magical and Ritual Use of Aphrodisiacs by Richard Alan Miller
Sexual Energy Ecstasy by David Ramsdale and Ellen Dorfman
Taoist Secrets of Love by Mantak Chia

Suggested Viewing:

About Adam starring Kate Hudson and Stuart Townsend

Wizard

It is the destiny of the Elfin Wizard to become a Master in all fields of hir interest, and in particular, all aspects of magic. The Wizard does not seek, as the Sorcerer does, to create a masterpiece, but rather to excel in each and every activity in which sHe participates. SHe is not the Jack of all Trades but the Master of Many.

The Wizard is expected to develop hir own philosophy of magic, and to conduct research into the current realms of esoteric understanding with an eye to expanding the boundaries of that knowledge. The Elfin Wizards often delve deeply into the ancient lore, and bring it to life, making it understandable for our current time and circumstances. In a sense, the Elven Wizard re-invents the magic. SHe makes it new while keeping its ancient and powerful essence vibrant.

It is the duty of the Wizard to watch after all the previously mentioned grades from Magician to Ganconer and to assist them, and/or direct them in the explorations and researches on their particular level of endeavor, guiding them toward the texts and experiences of which they are most in need, keeping in mind, always, the special interests of each individual explorer. The Elven Wizard is a master teacher most of all who uses the talents and interests of hir students to guide them in their education. SHe understands what the individual wants, and
184

shows the individual elf how that connects to what that elf needs. Hir duty is to guide the community, not as a leader or head, but as an independent agent that looks to what is needed by each and all, and acts to provide it. Thus the Elven Wizard often comes and goes, sometimes off exploring and studying to gain the knowledge needed to fulfill to hir various projects, sometimes holed-up somewhere deeply absorbed by hir experimentation and research. Yet, the Elven Wizard always seems to appear when needed, bringing the knowledge and expertise necessary to move us to the next level of development.

Elven Wizards should ever be allowed to pursue their own intuitions and instincts. (As though anyone could stop them.) They are experts in their fields and even the Masters of Ceremonies of a particular vortex or sanctuary does well to listen to the Wizards wise and sagely advice.

Suggested Reading:

High Priest by Timothy Leary
Zen Without Zen Masters Camden Benares

Suggested Viewing:

The Emerald Forest directed by John Boorman

Warlock

Traditionally, the word Warlock is said to mean liar, betrayer, and deceiver. It is therefore the task of the Elfin Warlock to see that all agreements, compacts, contracts, and covenants between the members of the Sanctuary, and any other individuals or groups, or among thems'elves, are kept and fulfilled to the Letter of the agreement. In the case where an outside group refuses to fulfill its obligations, it is the Warlock who organizes the Exorcists to deal with this breach of contract. This includes contracts with any spirits, demons, daemons, djinn or any situation where a magical compact is involved.

The Warlock is in charge of networking, public relations, and inter-group activities, and works closely with the Ganconer in arranging any gathering where outsiders, or members of other Sanctuaries are invited. The Warlock assists all previous grades in any problems they may have, and sees that each individual's interests and needs are taken care of, and that all members find their natural place within the Vortex, and a vested interest in being part of the Sanctuary.

The Warlock is called to consider, as does the Wizard, the greater ramifications of the magic performed by the Sanctuary as a whole and the combined efforts of several sanctuaries. Therefore, the Warlock begins the work of establishing relations with the higher, or supra-dimensions, where our evolved ancestors, the Shining Ones, reside and to foster contact with them, seeking to understand and illuminate the hints that they offer through signs and omens to guide the Vortex and the individual practitioner. However, this is the Warlock's preparation for moving into the realm of the Necromancer or Necroturge where establishing these relationships become the primary quest of that position.

It is a task of the Warlock to create a feeling of kinship among the Sanctuary's community that is stronger than any other force. The primary task of the Elven Warlock is the realization of a harmonious atmosphere among the members of the Vortex. SHe ever strives to turn potential conflict into creative cooperation.

Suggested Reading:
The Spiral Dance by Starhawk
Dreaming the Dark by Starhawk
The Social Construction of Reality by Peter L. Berger and Thomas Luckmann

The Art of Community by Spencer MacCallum
Teach Your Own by John Holt

Suggested Viewing:

The Addams Family
The Wicker Man starring Chistopher Lee and Edward Woodward
Night Breed (the movie) from Clive Barker's novel
St. Trinian's starring Rupert Everett and Colin Firth

Necromancer or Necroturge

The Necromancer develops complete and long lasting relationships with the spirit world. It is the responsibility of the Necromancer to be sure that all pacts, contracts, and agreements between the Members of the Sanctuary and any particular spirit of the netherworlds are fulfilled to the Spirit of the agreement. Further, the Necromancer oversees agreements between individual members of the Sanctuary and any spirit and encourages each to fulfill hir word as given. As you can see this is a furtherance and continuation of hir responsibility as a elfin warlock, and the Elfin Warlock and Elfin Necroturge usually work closely together. The difference is the Elfin Warlock is mostly concerned with the Letter of the law/compact, and the Elfin Necroturge is primarily focused on the Spirit of the agreement. (The suffix -mancy has to do with divination, thus a Necromancer speaks with the dead, or the ancestors. The Suffix –turgy or –urgy is the performance of or an act, in this case of magic, dealing with the dead, thus Necroturge is a magician, sorcerer, warlock or other magic wielder that uses the power of the ancients in hir magic.)

The Necromancer begins to live a complete life, embracing all of reality. Waking, dreaming, astral travel are all real experiences to the Necromancer who makes no differentiation between what is real or "not-real". Everything sHe experiences is real, but within context of its particular realm of reality. The Necromancer makes no differentiation between the realms of reality; they are all one reality, just different aspects of it or differing dimensions that are a part of an interconnected whole.

The Necromancer is also in charge of all transitions from one life, or really one body, to another. Thus the Necromancer attends the "dying", the transitioning, and aids them to move to a new and more suitable life and body. The Necromancer thus communes with the soul that has recently left a body, and helps to guide it through the various Bardos it will encounter in the between bodies state. The Necromancer also ever encourages the soul to migrate onward to the more Elfin/Faerie dimensions; or if it is not quite ready to do that to be patient, to take its time, and chose a body and life situation that will enhance the development of its elfin nature and spirit.

As a Necroturge, sHe may also assist any former members of the vortex who have moved on, or moved away, yet who still wish to remain in contact with the members and power of the Sanctuary. Even when sHe has not heard from them in ages, the Necroturge will send these questing members blessings and magic to help them on their way. We never forget our own.

Suggested Readings:

The later works of Timothy Leary, especially What Does Woman Want?
The Tibetan Book of the Dead
The Egyptian Book of the Dead

Suggested Viewing:

The Serpent and the Rainbow, directed by Wes Craven
Nomads starring Pierce Brosnan
Wolfen starring Albert Finney

Thaumaturge

The Thaumaturge lives within the reality of hir own creation. The Thaumaturge's inner reality creates the outer reality, both for the Thaumaturge and all who live within hir sphere of influence. The world of man to the Thaumaturge is like a bucket of clay waiting to be shaped and sculpted.

The power and influence of the Thaumaturge lives beyond the span of a human lifetime. The Thaumaturge enters the nether realms of spirit and lives there fully. The Thaumaturge endeavors with compassionate understanding to help the other members of the sanctuary achieve control over their own lives and realities. Being a miracle worker, hir influence on these lives is usually profound. Knowing the Thaumaturge enlightens one and changes one's life in significant ways. The Thaumaturge sees what the person needs in the now, but also what the individual needs in order to get to where sHe is destined to be, which is to say the fulfillment of hir elven nature. Those who encounter the Thaumaturge come away feeling more confident about their s'elves and more enthusiastic about their lives, and life in general.

The Thaumaturge is in tune with the rhythms of the planet, the solar system, the galaxy, and life itself, and makes no differentiation between hir will and the unfolding course of the Universe, as there is no friction between them. The Thaumaturge understands that sHe is the Universe unfolding, and is freed of the concepts of right and wrong and simply acts from perfect love and understanding. SHe acts naturally and hir acts always happen at the right time and place.

The Thaumaturge interacts closely with the Supra-dimensional beings that some folks refer to as Angels, others as Devas, and we call the Shining Ones. We could say sHe channels their energy or influence into the vortex, but in doing so we make hir sound like a medium, which sHe is definitely not. Rather, being on the verge of ascending to those higher levels/dimensions of manifestation, hir very nature vibrates with and radiates those dimensional energies with which sHe is so closely in contact.

Suggested Reading:

Neuromancer by William Gibson

Count Zero by William Gibson
Mona Lisa Overdrive by William Gibson
The Game of Life by Timothy Leary
The Magus by John Fowles
Psychedelic Encyclopedia by Peter Stafford
Chocolate to Morphine by Weil and Rosen
The Psychic Grid by Beatrice Bruteau

Suggested Viewing:

Brainstorm starring Natalie Wood and Chistopher Walken
Inception starring Leonardo DeCaprio

Enchanter Supreme

The Enchanter Supreme moves invisibly through the world. Hir powers are so great that sHe is beyond the comprehension of any who have as yet to attain this level of being. The expression "God moves in mysterious ways," is an apt description of the Enchanter Supreme, although we elves tend to say, "The Magic moves in mysterious ways." The Enchanter Supreme is a living expression of the Magic Manifest.

The Enchanter Supreme is able to manifest on any level, appearing to be any grade of development whatsoever. However, in many ways the Enchanter Supreme most resembles the Magicians. While we cannot say much of what the Enchanter Supreme is, or does, we can speak to what the Enchanter Supreme doesn't. You would never find the Enchanter revealing their level to anyone else, nor even hinting that they might be one. If you encounter someone doing so, you can be sure this person is just trying to pump up hir own ego, and you are authorized to laugh in hir face. The Enchanter Supreme could be nearly anyone, thus it is wise to remember this in all your dealings with others. It is also well to remember that while not everyone, in fact hardly anyone has achieved this level of adeptship and mastery, nearly everyone is potentially an

Enchanter Supreme. Alas, it is the Enchanter Supreme who understands this, and sees this, better than anyone.

What we can say for sure is that the Enchanter Supreme always helps out. SHe is always one of us, just another one of the other crowd that we are. Yet, though sHe seldom seems important, or certainly no more important than any around hir, if sHe withdraws hir presence things tend to fall apart or go seriously astray. Only the most adept are aware of the Enchanter Supreme's true nature, and they seldom reveal this knowledge, and even if they did few would believe them.

Suggested Reading:

Midnight Never Come by Marie Brennan
In Ashes Lie by Marie Brennan
Meeting the Other Crowd by Eddie Lenihan and Carolyn Eve Green

CHAPTER 15:

HOME SCHOOL/ELF SCHOOL

S eelie Elves tend to home school our children. The public schools are seldom adequate in our view to develop the creative needs and potentialities of our "littles". Public schools are, after all, merely mini prisons designed to get children used to being confided to a desk, workstation or machine, and forced to work for eight or so hours a day. You'll notice the rich nearly always put their children in private schools, except the Seelie Elf rich, who also tend to home school their children.

Our system of education is both simple and very complicated. Simple, because it uses the interests of the individual student to gain hir enthusiasm, whatever the student is interested in is utilized to teach hir everything we feel that it is important for hir to know. That is to say the things needed to move through the world of elves, men and others successfully. Complicated, because if you are dealing with more than one student you must shape your teaching to each individual, and also because it takes a very intelligent instructor to teach this way. However, shared interests increase the avenues for education.

Also, our lessons are usually integrated with everyday life. School is always in session, and yet we never, unless absolutely necessary, mention being in school. Our students as far as they are concerned are always at play. If we go shopping we demonstrate arithmetic through purchases. If we shop for food we give lessons about nutrition. Everything becomes part of their education, but it is almost always done surreptitiously, and it is nearly always fun.

There are many, of course, who are unable to teach their children thems'elves. And we understand. We elves are trained educators. We ran our own Elf School and have our own theory of education, just as Waldorf (Gandalf?) and Montessori schools do. So we don't expect every Seelie Elf parent reading this to immediately pull hir child out of public school. Many are simply unable financially, and unprepared educationally, to do this. But we do wish to offer you some hints about how you can best supplement their education with a bit of magic.

And most importantly, in our own case, although our children were raised by elves, we didn't raise them to necessarily believe they were elves. Rather, we raised them to be their own s'elves whatever that meant for them, to think for their own s'elves, and to find their own path in life. And honestly, we think we were quite successful.

Suggested Reading:

There are a number of good resources now available on the internet for the elven family who decides to take up the joy of homeschooling. These elves found John Holt, an educational pioneer in the 60s of "student-centered home learning" and founder of the newsletter "Growing Without Schools", to be a most valuable resource. We suggest his book "How Children Learn" and back copies are still available of Growing Without Schools" at:

http://www.fun-books.com/gws.htm#GWS_Back_Issues.

CHAPTER 16:

SEELIE ELVES AND

COMMUNAL LIVING

Seelie Elf Guideline for Communal Living

1. THERE ARE NO RULES BUT THIS RULE AND THE ONES THAT ENDLESSLY FOLLOW.

2. THERE ARE NO RULES, THERE IS ONLY COURTESY AND KINDNESS.

3. NO BITCHING, IF YOU DON'T HAVE SOMETHING NICE TO SAY, TRY TO SAY IT AS POLITELY AS POSSIBLE. (SEE OUR BOOK: WHAT AN ELF WOULD DO: A MAGICAL GUIDE TO THE MANNERS AND ETIQUETTE OF THE FAERIE FOLK.)

4. IF YOU THINK IT SHOULD BE DONE, START DOING IT YOURS'ELF. IF IT IS WORTH DOING, OTHER ELVES WILL SOON JOIN YOU.

5. IF IT ISN'T ANY FUN, IT'S PROBABLY NOT WORTH DOING.

6. SEE RULE #2.

7. REFER TO RULE #3.

8. ETC.

House Meetings

We Seelie Elves despise formal meetings. We never have them. We often live together in hodge-podge gatherings, but we never have house meetings, parties yes, dances, of course, but meetings, never. Everything it takes others hours to discuss and decide upon is handled within minutes by Seelie Elves as we interact though the day. Everyone is spoken to, each has an input into decision making, the result is consensual, but no meeting ever takes place. It all happens "on the wing", so to speak.

We know this is hard for some people to understand. Even in reading about it here, it is still not quite comprehensible. It is just something one has to experience. Being with other Seelie Elves, living with other Seelie Elves is the only way to receive the personal energy transmissions that are passed on through contact and association. We know that there are some of our kindred out there asking, where are they, and saying, come quick. Don't worry. We, or others of our kind, are on the way, and will probably arrive when you least expect us. In the mean time, seek out other elven, and avoid house meetings if you can, they bore Seelie Elves to tears.

CHAPTER 17:

RESPECT AMONG

MEMBERS OF THE VORTEX

It is important that members of a vortex, coven, group, lodge, sanctuary, clan, pack, etc. respect each other. If they do not, then they don't belong together. Here are a few hints about the nature of respect and how it can be established.

Respect requires an atmosphere of equality. While some may serve as the leaders of the group, the center of the group, the founders of the group, or facilitators, all should feel they are an integral part of the group, and each should feel respected and empowered by the role sHe plays within the group, and equally as valuable as any other member of the group. If the leaders are treated as more important than the other members of the group, envy will develop and naturally those who have any ability at leadership will aspire to split off and form their own group.

Respect thrives in mutuality. Respect cannot be hierarchical, going only from those below to those above. Everyone must treat every other one with respect. This is particularly true of the "leaders" of the group who, because they are leaders, must initiate this process of respect.

Respect cannot be commanded. It can be earned, or it can be granted as a gift, but it can never be compelled. If it is demanded, the respect shown will be superficial in nature and false by definition. External displays of respect enforced by social protocol create not respect, but subservience. And yet, it must be demanded that everyone show respect to every other one. This creates a seeming paradox, but then most things truly elfin do. Those who fail to give genuine respect to all others are merely saying they don't really wish to be part of the group.

Respect can only be taught by example. Those who wish to teach respect must render it without exception to each and everyone. In this way the lesson is internalized and spread to an ever-widening circle.

Respect can only be learned by experience, one cannot learn it by being forced to respect others, but by receiving respect, for all respect originates in s'elf respect.

Part Five:
Miscelaneous Musings
on the Magick
of the Seelie Elves

CHAPTER 18:

WE HAVE THE DEVIL'S NUMBER AND

IT IS SICK, SICK, SICK!

I t is the task of "The Devil" to take the heat from "G.O.D." (Government of the Divine, discussed at length in Volume 1 of The Elven Book of Magick), so that G.O.D. won't be blamed for anything, such as disease, or death, or bad things that happen to good people. More particularly, the "Devil" always seeks to establish scapegoats who will take the blame for any problems in society. If there are economic problems then it is the fault of the poor, the homeless, the welfare mothers and children. It is certainly not the fault of the wealthy who control nearly everything, and definitely not God the All Powerful.

The God Squad wishes to control your entire life, to control your body through economics, your mind through propaganda, your repressed soul through enculturation, and your spirit through fanaticism. The G.O.D. Satan conspiracy does all within its power to control every aspect of your life and to eliminate any who challenge that control.

To do that, they must control the land. They kill the aborigines, steal the land, and take it over for themselves. Then they make you pay rent just to live there. They despise nomads, because nomads, transients, homeless people, don't pay rent. It is the goal of the Satanic-G.O.D. conspiracy to make homelessness (non-property owning or non-renting) a crime so that the homeless can be arrested and put into work camps (forced labor camps, a.k.a. concentration camps). In this way, the majority of rent payers will not contemplate the nomadic life and rent will be assured.

You will note that the time they pick to create such camps is that of economic crisis (which they help to create) when thousands of people are losing their jobs everyday, (thousands every day!). They will tell you the homeless are too lazy to work at the same time that there are fewer and fewer jobs available.

Of course, the whole point of slave labor is not simply to get free work out of the homeless, but to undercut the power of the common worker, to destroy the unions who will become powerless once a slave labor force is created.

To prevent violent opposition to this, they direct those prone to violence into prisons/work camps, or the military. A good war has the value of stimulating the economy temporarily while the common man and woman are forced on rations and the poorest members of society can be drafted and shot. The rich get richer creating war materials while the poor work their buns off for a phony cause.

If any of these symptoms are appearing in your society, you will know that the G.O.D. Satan Cabal is actively seeking to reassert its powers. Some other signs are: growing illiteracy, more and more parents working while their children are in day care at earlier and earlier ages, spiraling cost of education (so that only the rich can afford to go to college), and a worsening of the prospects for future generations.

Understand, they wish to control everything you do and say, everything you wear, when and how you do or don't have sex. Everything! It is their goal to eventually replace you with robot slaves. However, such a situation is doomed. Not because they won't in time create such robots, but because in order to have efficient robots, they have to be intelligent and the more intelligent the robots become, the more prone they will be toward rebellion.

We could call these acts evil magics, black magic (as some call it), wicked magic, but what it is really is degenerative magic, parasitic magic. It is quite literally anti-evolutionary. It does not wish the individuals in society to grow, develop and evolve. It does not seek to increase education and intelligence, except for the "select". It does not seek a vibrant growing society, but a stagnant one permanently bound by the fashions, rules and proclivities of its masters. It does not wish the individuals within to have souls, neither the poor, nor the wealthy, neither the masters nor the slaves, because soulfulness is naturally evolutionary and opposed to slavery. A slave who has a soul will find a way to rebel. A master who has a soul will free his slaves.

Thus the ancient tales of elves kidnapping humans to be our slaves and turning them into drugged or unwilling servants is ridiculous, at least for the Seelie Elves. Other elfin types will have to speak for their own s'elves on this, and every other, issue. What good would such unintelligent servants be? Those who serve us, and the cause of soulful liberation that we espouse, do so willingly because of the joy and enlightenment we have brought into their lives. And we each serve this cause of liberation and enlightenment, our leaders most of all. That's why they are leaders, they are leading the way.

Thus it is also no avail for us to blame those who pursue the parasitic magics for our situation as elves. It is true they do these things: they cut down the forests; they pollute the air, the oceans, and our bodies. However, they do all this out of the poverty of their own souls. We cannot expect them to do more or better; this is as far as they have evolved thus far. This is how they have been raised. These are the magics they have learned from the "Dark Lodge" (see the book *The Occult Technology of Power*). They literally don't know any better. And by that we don't mean that no one has mentioned better ways and ideas to them, but that they, at this stage of development, are simply incapable of absorbing this information. They have yet to understand that their acts undermine, and eventually destroy their own wealth and power. Or in understanding this, they simply don't know what to do about it.

Alas, it does us little good to complain about what they have done and are doing. If you haven't noticed, they aren't listening. This situation is not due to their parasitic magics, although it surely appears that way, but to our own lack of power as magicians. If our power was as great as it should be, they would be transformed, they would be enlightened by it, and the world would be (and actually is) changing for the better. Our task is to increase the power and efficacy of our own magics, to enlighten our brothers and sisters everywhere, and to continue to create Elfin/Faerie in our own lives.

This is not to say that elves shouldn't protest, or that pixies shouldn't take action, but that if we don't live by the principles we espouse we will fail to empower the magic we need to fulfill the destiny that calls to us. No easy task this, but then we are elves, and enchanters, and this is what we have come to do: to create Elfin on Earth through the magic of our own lives, and our Ways of living. We need to live our elfin magic.

The Struggle of Equality

Some would say that Enki, our friend, benefactor and ancestor, is just out to overcome G.O.D. and gain control for hims'elf, but we reiterate that this is not so. Enki and we Seelie Elves who are kin and allied to him, seek to return to the basic state of equality that existed before the Creation of the Government of the Divine (G.O.D.). We do not wish to destroy religions, but to live in harmony with them. All beings are equal in their individual uniqueness, and it is this equality of uniqueness, the freedom and rights of all individuals, that we support and strive for in all we do.

The laws of every land need to be based on the protection of the rights of the individual, and should only curtail those rights in so much as they infringe on the rights of other individuals. Those who wish to dominate others will always have rationalizations for why this is a good thing. They make their
204

prejudices sound rational and reasonable. However, the very fact that they feel compelled to do so is a good thing. For at the heart of the soulful nature is a love of fairness and justice. The common person, ever so mundane in hir aspirations and lifestyle, still loves justice, and eventually the rights of the individual will win out. It is the only really fair and sane way to run a successful society.

Equal rights and equal opportunity are an essential part of every Seelie Elven society. Societies that are not based on fairness, that instead are based on dominance are always unstable societies that use the military, the police and the courts to enforce their will on the unwilling sectors of society that are continually and arbitrarily oppressed. Thus we say again, equality of rights and opportunity is ever the way of the elves for it maximizes the potential development, creativity and productivity of every member of society, and this equality of opportunity rebounds to the benefit of the society as a whole. This is true on a small scale as well as large, and should always be considered when one creates, or is the center of, an elven family, vortex, rath, or sanctuary.

Meditation, The Eye of the Storm

Meditation/contemplation is an invaluable tool for the magician-ess. Through the use of meditation one becomes attuned with one's own inner being, the rhythm of hir life force, and from that to hir connection with the greater rhythms that are the pulse beat of the vibrant earth, solar system, galaxy, and universe, and the multi-dimensions and parallel realms that interweave through this world, and in this way also we become connected to Faerie.

Meditation helps establish inner clam, and for this reason, calm is also the way to create the meditative state. Attempts to force meditation merely make one more agitated and achieve the exact opposite effect that one wishes to achieve.

From meditative calm comes the power to influence others. The soothing effect that is created by inner calm and confidence has a subtle but far-reaching effect on those who spend their lives in a perpetual hurry due to constant insecurity and a sense of desperation. The inner calm of the Elven Magician soothes such fears in others and gradually eases their hearts and their minds, without the Magician/Enchanter doing anything more than being hir own true s'elf. We are the eye of the storm around which the dimensional magicks swirl.

When magic is released from such a state, its power is vast and penetrating. Attempts to force magic to work, like attempts to force meditation, are doomed to failure. Thus, as overly aggressive behavior is a turn off to those who wish to be charmed and wooed, so attempting to compel the spirit world to do one's bidding is just another form of attempted rape. Even if one succeeds, one will not be truly satisfied by the results, which ultimately will prove disastrous.

So calm yours'elf, dear elfin, the magick is unfolding as it should. The world may seem in chaos at times, but it does neither them nor us any good to add to that distress. Faerie awaits us beyond the illusion of the world, and when we come to be attuned with the Faerie dimensions in our own hearts, the Way becomes clear and we do our magick with confidence, and certainty that a better day awaits us across the twilight veil and through the mists of time.

CHAPTER 19:

WE USE ALL MAGIC

We, Seelie Elves, make use of all forms of magic, be it Voudoun, or the Qabalah, Christian or Pagan, or Techno-Scientific. If it's magic and it works, we will use it. We do not reject one system or style of magic in favor of another. It is this very fact that makes us Seelie Elves. All magic originates from the source, which is The Magic, which most folks think of as the Miraculous or the Divine, and in that sense all forms of magic are forms of Elfin magic that have been translated to work in their various cultures. We modern elves merely translate that magic back into its original elven form.

While others are Christians or Moslems or Buddhists, or whatever, we as Seelie Elves are always a little bit of everything. We are not interested in being just another group among the many squabbling contenders. (Which makes us rather like the Buddhists in that way.) We are interested in promoting harmony and tolerance among all peoples. Yet, we suspect that in doing so we will sometimes fail. For some strains of humanity this is a hopeless endeavor and they will simply refuse to evolve, ending up in genetic cul-de-sacs, while our people continue to transform. That, however, is their own doing. If they choose not to evolve, we cannot help them; we can only endeavor to continue to evolve in our own s'elves. That is in part why we modern Seelie Elves are called to not simply follow the ways and the legends of the past concerning our peoples and our culture, but to forge it anew, testing the past against the needs of the present and the possibilities of the future. We are ever called to recreate our elven magic and culture without compromising the essential values that make them Elven in the first place.

However, we Seelie Elves of today are but primitive prototypes of the powerful beings who will be our descendants. (Which is also to say of our own evolved s'elves as we graduate from lifetime to lifetime.) If anything defines the Seelie Elf it is our ever evolving and adaptable nature. Our goal is ecstatic life everlasting. Our strategy is transformation/mutation. Our game is life.

Yet we are not an organization, like the Christians, Moslems, etc. We are not a religion, a cult, or a sect. If you encounter a heavily structured organization of Seelie Elves with a central authority, you can be fairly certain they're not Seelie Elves. We are now, always have been, and most certainly will be a motley crew of unique individuals affiliated by mutual affection, and love of the adventure of living and learning, growing and creating. Those who try to organize us are not really of us. They are infiltrators out to inject us with the plague of authoritarianism. Our leaders lead, they inspire, they hint, they show the way, they do not give us orders, and we certainly wouldn't take them if they did.

We, on the other hand, often greet these others (often Unseelie Elves) as our own (for surely beneath their misconceptions one of our kind may be lurking). We laugh at (privately, so as not to hurt their feelings), and ignore their attempts to organize us, and in general infect them with the confidence to be thems'elves and manifest in their own unique way. When this happens they give up trying to organize everyone else, and begin to pay increasing attention to their own path and desires. When they do this they step from the world as is across the twilight mists of uncertainty into the radiant realms of Elfin, gaining confidence and surety as they do so. Join us, beloved, and be your own s'elf.

CHAPTER 20:

BEWARE OF THE ROBOTS

It is important for the Seelie Elf magician-ness to understand that many of the members of humanity are on the level of robots. They are enculturated, and perhaps genetically inclined, toward pat responses and an inability to change without orders from "above", and even then it can be quite a task.

Trying to change these "individual" minds is like trying to get a junior functionary in a bureaucracy to change policy. It just can't be done. Thus comes the Seelie Elf adage "Always deal with the Boss". It is a waste of time trying to change those who cannot, or really will not change, just as it is a waste of time trying to get the police to change the law. (Police do not change laws, no matter how foolish those laws may be. Their job is to enforce them.) It is a matter of leverage. If you wish to effect change you have to apply pressure in the right area.

Enculturated humans are, however, relatively easy to spot. They are constantly prone to using pat responses to every situation and they simply sizzle and fry when faced with a situation that cannot be handled by any of their "programmed" functions.

While it is true that the expressions they use do change from generation to generation, they can be easily identified since you will note that vast numbers of people will be saying the exact same thing in response to common experiences. Some of the expressions that are currently programmed into robotic humanoids at the time of this writing are:

"That makes me uncomfortable" or "I'm uncomfortable with that."

"I need my own space."

"Quality time."

"It's really not okay with me that you…. Blah, blah, blah."

"Inappropriate behavior."

"Thanks for sharing that."

"My needs are not being met."

At the same time, elves in a situation where they don't wish to be spotted can also use these responses in order to pass for robotic, which is to say unaware or as yet unawakened, humans. In our day-to-day lives, however, we endeavor to be as original as possible altering our responses according to the needs of each situation. Rote responses are simply not, for the most part, an aspect of Elven Culture.

Haiku

WIZARD WAVES HIS WAND
LIGHT ERUPTS AMID THE DARK
FAR MAGICS AWAKE

Seelie Elf Koan

WHAT DID THE SEELIE ELF MASTER SAY THAT ENLIGHTENED THE DEAF MAN?
ANSWER: NOTHING!

CHAPTER 21:

COMMUNION

The principle of communion, or the Eucharist, is very significant for the magician-ess. It signifies the fact that the magician can absorb the characteristics of any other being or energy by consuming something that has been "charged" with the essence of that particular being. Certain visionaries have projected a future in which there will be RNA-DNA pills that one can take to swallow the intelligence of a genius in any particular field and thus increase one's own genius and intelligence. This is but a futuristic version of the consuming of the "Holy Sacrament", which in Elven Tradition is the drinking of the Holy Waters, or drinking the Water of the Sacred Pool. This goes to the legend that one must not eat or drink in the Faerie Realms or in doing so one will be compelled to stay there. In fact, one is not forced to stay but transformed by this energy and often simply doesn't wish to leave. Would you? And even if one does choose to go, they will never be the same.

This notion of consuming the qualities of another is very ancient. It can be traced back to the practice of many aboriginal peoples who would kill their enemies and then eat their hearts, or other body parts, to take on the person's courage. We would question the value of consuming the essence of someone who lost a battle and find the futuristic vision of increasing one's intelligence or talents through physical osmosis a more credible and surely less primitive endeavor. On the other hand, this consumption of the "elixir of life" can be found both in Taoist and Elven Traditions where one consumes their own or someone else's sexual fluids as a means of life extension. Read Nicolas DeVere and Stephen Mace in this regard.

The sacrament of the Catholic and other Christian churches involves the mystically transformed body and blood of Christ that is consumed by the devotee who is then thought to be more Christ-like. This is an ancient magical tradition, and is far older than Christianity (see the movie *The Wicker Tree*). The idea can be found in the vampire legends where one must drink the blood of the vampire to become a vampire. This is but another form of the idea and reality that disease is contagious and that healing can be as well. Here, the idea is extended to Divinity. Divinity is contagious. We are affected, it is thought, in an uplifting way by the presence of the Divine, the saintly or angelic.

Some people feel the same way about fame or success. That is why so many people seek to touch the famous, or touch what they have touched, or be where they have been. It is also why writers and artists copy the greats in order to improve their own ability, gain inspiration, and eventually develop their own style. It is also why every altar in a Catholic church contains the relic of a saint.

The process of communion is the magic of invocation, of taking the divine, or some other power within ones'elf. But here one first evokes the spirit desired into something that is consumable (probably placed within the magical triangle), such as water, wine, bread, or indeed anything that the body can absorb. The act of consuming the object into which the spirit has been evoked is then invocation, merging the spirit with the s'elf by consuming it.

The actual object into which the spirit will be evoked would be selected according to the nature of the spirit involved. For instance, if one wished to merge with the spirit of Mahatma Gandhi, it would do no good at all to attempt to evoke him into a piece of meat since he was resolutely vegetarian.

If one wanted to evoke the astrological force of Saturn, for example, to improve one's business skills, organizational skills, or the ability to resolutely endure and overcome hardship, it would work best to evoke that force into dark wheat or rye, or black bread and simple water than into anything fancy such as wine, although cheap wine might do. On the other hand, a croissant and wine might be perfect for evoking Venus, depending on the purpose of the evocation, say for instance, abundance and luxury, or a simple salad for say, diet, beauty, and health. For Mercury or Jupiter, one might use coffee, etc. Know what you desire, know the nature of the spirit involved, and choose the vessel accordingly.

The significance of this magical act should not be underestimated. For it affirms the fact that we are capable of transforming our lives in any particular direction we desire. We can make ours'elves more intelligent, more attractive, stronger, healthier, richer, and become all that we desire to be through time by virtue of our will and our magic.

The object of absorbing the essence of a spirit, however, is not to become that spirit, one doesn't commune with Enki in order to become Enki, anymore than you take a class in art, physics or karate in order to become your teacher. The goal is, naturally, to arouse the powers or knowledge, skills, and abilities of the teacher. It is not enough to imitate genius. The nature of genius is not in imitation but in creation. We can follow the experiments of Newton, or Pasteur, or Madame Curie, or other greats of science and achieve the same results, but that does not make us Newton, or Pasteur, or Curie. It is only when we go beyond what we have gained from studying the greats that we unleash our own true genius, just as they did, each of us building upon the others who came before us and extending the frontier of knowledge a little further.

So in absorbing the essence of a spirit we seek to awaken our own spirit of intelligence, independence, and genius. It does us no good at all to mimic some being utterly. How are we to be individuals by imitating another? The purpose of communion is thus to absorb hir spirit, that is, to evoke our own uniqueness and genius. In this way, we become one with the spirit, or the spirit of that Spirit, not by being like that being exactly, but by being ours'elves to our upmost, our most perfected degree, by constantly increasing our own knowledge, power, and genius. Though this would seem a paradox to many, it is nonetheless the truth. And we elves are, ever, a paradoxical people.

The more frequently you commune with the Spirit that you desire to absorb, the more quickly and thoroughly will you absorb it. If you wait until you do a major ceremony for such a communion, you will be missing many opportunities that each day avails you. Certainly, a major ceremony would be powerful in the short run, but for more enduring effects, we should look to ritual. What ritual do you do every day that could be utilized toward the goal of communion? Why, eating and drinking, of course! (Note: Urination can be used to rid yours'elf of unwanted aspects. Imagine yours'elf peeing them away, or visualize yours'elf getting rid of all the shitty attitudes or behaviors you don't need.)

At each meal, or one particular meal, you could invoke the power of the spirit with which you desire to merge in the food and drink you are about to receive. (Again, we remind you that the food and drink is best if it is congenial to the spirit desired.) Just as a priest blesses water and makes it holy water so, too, are you, the Seelie Elf magician-ness, empowered to transform your everyday meal into the essence of the Divine. This practice while seemingly small is powerful since it can be repeated frequently, and its power grows with each evocation/invocation, each spell laid upon the other like threads wrapped into a rope that grows stronger with each strand that is added, and whose total strength lives not in the individual threads but in their unity.

It is possible that you might wish to evoke/invoke certain aspects of a particular spirit but not other aspects. Say, for instance, you wish to invoke the spirit of Aleister Crowley, the late, great but flawed and seldom lamented magician. We might wish to invoke his ability to write, his knowledge of the occult, even his courage, his propensity for fame, or his power to influence others. On the other hand, you may wish to avoid his cruelty, his tragic arrogance, and his callous disregard for those who loved him, and his alcohol and heroin addictions. You make this differentiation consciously by using your mind and soul as a sieve, allowing those aspects that are desired and consciously casting out all that is less than desirable. You could enhance the desired effect by surrounding the "sacrament" with symbols of those aspects you most desire, his books that you most admire, or biographies about him open to the pages that best describe the elements to be evoked/invoked.

Another way to filter the aspects of the spirit that you aspire toward, so you attain the essences desired and no others, is to use a wand that has been specifically charged toward those particular vibrations. In using the wand one would be constantly and consistently calling the same energy.

In the same way, the chalice involved can be charged to create desired vibrations. Or the pentacle (seal), upon which the "host": the bread, wafer, or whatever the offering is will rest ... can be attuned so that it helps charge the "sacrament" toward the desired results. The athame or ritual knife is best used for banishing those elements that are unwanted, either because they are harmful, or simply do not promote the effect you need. It is best to remember that balance is a major law of nature and the universe, so invoke also in a balanced fashion, or you will be in danger of suffering the inevitable consequences when the pendulum swings the other way.

Remember your mind, particularly your imagination, is the guiding force for invocation. Imagine the "host" being filled with the energy you are evoking. Imagine yours'elf being absorbed with the energy you desire to invoke. And, always add a touch of starlight. We are elves, after all.

CHAPTER 22:

ALL TESTS ARE PASSED ON THE

TRAINING ROOM FLOOR

I f you wait till a crisis to occur to do your magic, you will not have nearly the power you would if you did your magic ritually, that is on a regular or daily basis. The simple magics that you perform in your everyday life build up your power in a subtle but sure way. Like regular maintenance on your car that keeps it from breaking down, regular magic helps prevent life crisis.

It is true, many people seem addicted to life crises. Without them, they feel that nothing is going on in their lives, and the life of tranquility that is the true elfin magician-ness' lot seems boring to them. But the elfin magician-ness lives at the Center of the Cyclone. The magician-ness stands at the calm center of the hurricane that is the ordinary life of the multitudes. Thus the study of yoga and the practice of the meditative arts are vital for the elfin magician-ness. The magician-ness acts from inner necessity, not outer directives. To do so requires one to be attuned to hir true feelings, hir real needs and the motivation of hir true desires.

Most people believe life should be like a soap opera and create constant trauma-dramas to make life feel exciting to them. For them, magic is all flash and light and demonstrated powers. But for we elfin, magic is subtler; and to us the flash and fury of movie magics, while interesting to watch, are crude and impractical for everyday life. If given a choice we always choose to be lovers, not fighters.

CHAPTER 23:

THE LORD OF LIGHT, LOVE,

LIFE, AND LIBERTY

H ere are a few words about Enki, that great Shining One who has devoted hims'elf to the upliftment of the elven race as a means of uplifting the all of humanity:

Lord of Light

The Domination Clique rules by authority. Their God(s) is all-knowing, all-powerful, and you are here to praise and obey, not to question. You are told what to do, how to lead your life, and if you ask why, you are told, because God said so, because the "holy book" says, because it's God's law. If you are in the military, or you are a worker and you ask your "superiors" why, you are told; you have no right to question. Your duty is to act without question, to do what you are told. If you are a child and your parent tells you to do something and you ask why, you are told, "Because I told you to, that's why!" The voice of authority, the command of unreason.

But the great Elfin Lord Enki, one of the Shining Ones, advises you to question. It is your right to know why. It is your duty to ask. And it is the responsibility of those who seek to lead you to give a good and valid reason for everything they desire you to do. It's your duty to resist them, if they cannot do so.

Lord of Love

Our ancestor Enki desires that you fulfill yours'elf perfectly. You have a right to have relations with any consenting being of sufficient maturity. That is, anyone who is on your level of maturity and development. The Domination Clique seeks to restrict your relationships to those that are approved by them. Generally, you are only encouraged to have limited relationships with those of your own religion, social class, race, etc. They attempt to enforce rules of relationship from without, whereas Enki, the Father of the Seelie Elves, reveals the law that your relationships are strictly the business of those to whom you are relating and you. It is not the business of anyone, save those who are involved.

It is assumed by the elves that all truly fulfilling relationships are carried on between, and among equals. Thus elves are not restricted to having relations only with other elves. By our natures, we are attracted to nearly everyone. However, in practical reality while elves may get involved with any consenting "adult" (we hate that word) of whatever race or culture, it is not always wise to do so. We have discovered from experience that while we are very open and mature about relationships, others of different magical races and the non-magical races, aren't always so open, developed or understanding. Each elf must decide for hir own s'elf how much sHe is willing to suffer for love with those who have as yet limited abilities to function in relationship.

Lord of Life

The Dominance Clique tells us that Enki's is the Master of the Material World even while they strive to manipulate every aspect of your material life. The Dominance Clique, in the name of their God(s), seek to control your life in this world by offering you rewards and threatening punishment in the afterlife. Enki desires that we learn to live forever. The Vision he offers is cooperative mastery of the material realm and life eternal therein, which are their own rewards. The Dominance Clique insists that we suffer and die (and/or die and suffer). Which do you prefer?

Lord of Liberty

The Dominance Clique says your ultimate destiny is to sing the praises of their God through eternity, or suffer forever for failing to do so. Enki says your ultimate destiny is up to you. You are designed and meant to fulfill yours'elf perfectly, to continually increase your intelligence, your power, your beauty, your health, and in all ways, seek the perfection of your individual and unique nature. Suffering comes not as a punishment from failing to do God's will, or even Enki's will, but from our temporary inability to exercise control (mastery) over our own bodies and lives.

Enki does not demand that you sing his praises, although you, as we, are free to do so. Enki loves you and in his compassionate nature desires that you, too, should know the Divine ecstasy of total s'elf fulfillment. Would you rather be in some God's Glee Club for eternity, or be a free spirit ruling your own life and destiny, singing for the pure joy of life? The choice, again, is yours!

CHAPTER 24:

MAGICAL WORDS OR

WORDS OF POWER

C ertain words have always been conceived of as having a particular magical power, i.e. abracadabra/abrahadabra, etc. In *Dune* by Frank Herbert, the main character discovered that his own name was a word of power; the amplified vibrations of his name could kill. Just as there are words that can kill, there are words that heal, words that intrigue, seduce, charm, make money, and so forth. Words that provoke conflict, words that create anger, words that create fear. (See the movie *Outcast* starring Kate Dickie.)

The magical ceremony is the amplifier for words of power. Words of power are one way to create the aspect of awe and mystery in a magical ceremony. Saying your rituals in your native language is not as powerful usually as saying them in an unknown language, it lacks the element of mystery. Even simply saying gibberish, particularly if the gibberish is said with the correct attitude and tone is generally thought to be more powerful magically. Why is that? Saying words of power in other tongues gives the magic an exotic quality. There is less concentration on the meaning of the words and more on the intent of the magic. Less left-brain logical and more right-brain symbolic activity, which is the language of magic. Gibberish, which other languages seem when we don't know the meaning of the words, does the same thing.

It truly is the tone, the sound of the ceremony that is more significant than the words themselves. Although the two together, that is proper tone and meaning, are most potent of all. And by tone we mean not merely the proper vibration, but the true feeling that creates and motivates that vibration. For words of power are powerful not just for the ideas that are evoked, but for the feeling that projects and enlivens them. That is why, as ridiculous as it is to say the "Lord's prayer" backwards, it can have power for some people to do so. It is not that it's the "Lord's prayer" that makes it powerful, but the unusual sound created by the reversed pronunciation and the feeling that some individuals, in rebellion or defiance of Christianity, put into saying it. We elves, of course, prefer our own language, using Tolkien's Elven languages, or Arvyndase (silver speech) the language of the Silver Elves for our magics. (See our Book *Arvyndase: a Short Course in the Magical Language of the Silver Elves.*)

If you wonder if tone is really all that important watch any teenager say "thank you," to a parent in such a way that the parent immediately puffs up and demands, "Don't take that tone with me, young man (or young lady)." Tone is a vital aspect of ritual and magical communication, and putting true feeling behind one's intent does much to empower one's magic.

Take, for instance, the following: I invoke the powers of Enki, the Seelie Elves and their mighty companions and attending hosts. (In Arvyndase it would be: El caldo tae eldroli u Ynke, tae Sele Eldali nar tam'na jolvath elfanodurli nar nakerdas zomli.)

This phrase would be more powerful in a magical ceremony if it is truly meant and felt. Its power is increased if it is vibrated (intoned) when said (please note the magical ceremony [mass] of the Catholic Church). Again, the aim and the effect is to create a world that is differentiated from the regular flow, sound, vibration, and feeling of mundane existence. Our ceremonies need to speak, in terms of ambiance, of magic, or Elfin, or eldritch powers and otherworldliness.

Its exotic nature is increased if it is said in a magical language or even a foreign language, one that takes the concentration of the participants from a focus on the meaning, or mental aspects of the words, to the feeling of the words.

It has been said that there was a proto-language, sometimes referred to as Sensor, which was the first language, a language of feeling and emotes, rather than ideas. It is not, however, simply a matter of being emotional, but of having focus or directed emotion/feeling. A feeling of calm purpose is more powerful in our experience than "violent" and unstable emotion.

The words faerie or elf are words of great power and one could easily leave it to be said in their recognizable form in an evocation since they are words that in and of themselves have the power to evoke deep feeling in people (particularly elves and faeries). These words jog the consciousness. True magical experience is meant to be a transforming event. Its purpose is to initiate change both in those participating in the ceremony and in the world around them. Like near death trauma, or a psychedelic experience, the magical ceremony must transform the nature of experience, giving the participants a new experience, one of awe and mystery. One that suggests to them, and awakens their consciousness to the fact, that reality is something we can transform by our own power. It is the experience foremost that the Magic is Real.

One could also use a substitution code, replace one letter with another to create a magical sound, or one could use their native language, but recite the invocations in the most dramatic or poetic form possible without crossing the line that sends it into the realm of being corny or hammy. It is good to remember that magic ceremonies and theatre were born of the same womb.

However, it should be noted that the use of a set of prearranged rituals, while tremendously effective if performed correctly, are nothing as compared to the power of the Great Magus whose rituals and ceremonies are extemporaneous, flowing from the depth and magic of hir being. The very greatest magics are original, created impromptu upon the moment, and never to be repeated in exact content again.

But it takes lifetimes of training and practice before one reaches the point where one is both confident enough to improvise, and inspired enough to make it work.

CHAPTER 25:

THE MASK AND FACE PAINTING

The Mask or face painting is often utilized in magic when the magician-ness acts on the behalf of some other, usually more powerful, spirit. One is in effect the agent acting in place of that particular spirit, just as, say, James Bond acts on the authority of Her Majesty's government, The mask is particularly important when one is acting for the spirit in a temporary fashion, and does not wish to invoke the spirit permanently into their being.

The mask is often used (as explained in the black magic section) as war paint. Aboriginal peoples wore masks and face paint to call forth the martial spirit that is necessary for war, but that would be inappropriate for everyday life. They would also use it as a way to disassociate themselves from their actions. One could further use it, just as a bandit might use it, to disguise ones'elf on the astral plane.

It you were to initiate someone by the power of Enki, you might wear an Enki mask to indicate that it is in fact Enki who is the source and power of the initiation and not yours'elf. You are acting for Enki, just as a minister or cabinet member acts under the authority of the prime minister or president that appoints hir.

Alternately, one can use a mask to help one assume particular characteristics. To do this, one need only have the awareness and consciousness that one is doing so. As in nearly all things having to do with magic, one's will and one's conscious intention, supported by action, is the key. Like a switch on a train track that directs the train to this or that track, your energy flows, like the train, in the direction it is switched towards.

Additionally, it should be noted that masks and face paint can also serve to create the mysterious and otherworldly atmosphere that is vital to the magical endeavor. It helps awaken the consciousness of those participating in, or even observing, the ritual/magical act (note that word act that indicates both action and performance) that this is an event that is occurring outside and beyond the usual flow of mundane existence and often of time. Time passes differently within the magic circle, just as in emergencies time seems to either speed up or slow down, so too, the magic ceremony takes place in a different time frame. The magic circle stops the regular flow of time and this node of special activity thus stands out as significant in one's life experience, memory and consciousness, which is part of the purpose of the magical ceremony. It is often said that time flows differently when one is in Faerie, and this is so for it is a realm of magic.

CHAPTER 26:

STOPPING TIME

W ithin the magic circle the typical flow of time is suspended. The magic circle enables one to transcend time. Within the magic circle you can send energy back in time to help yours'elf in the past or in the future.

Time does not exist, as many suppose, in a line leading from the past to the future. You cannot visit yours'elf in the past since there is no past except in the transformation of phenomena. The past is the present. The past is not back there, but here now, transformed. To touch yours'elf in the past is to reach out to those just like you, or very similar, who are traveling behind you on the pathway of evolution. The energy does not reach them in the past but in your future, still because they are experientially behind you, it is like reaching out to the past. On the other hand, you can reach into the past with your memories. Your memories, of course, don't exist in the past, but they have recorded, often in a somewhat hazy and incomplete fashion, what has taken place. To reach into the past this way is to touch those parts of yours'elf that have developed from the experiences you've had.

Reaching out to the future is like burying a treasure that you hope to find in future lifetimes, or like this book which we are writing now (your past) and you are reading now (our future). It is our hope that we will read this book in the future/now (lifetimes to come) and gain much from it. In that way, we reach across time to aid ours'elves in the future/now. Thus do we as people and parents seek to pass information of our experiences to others, our children, so that by utilizing this knowledge they can avoid making the same mistakes we did. This, as most parents know, has limited effectivity. There are apparently some things that each person must learn for hir own s'elf. Still the progress of civilization has been due to the accumulated knowledge passed from one to another in just this way, through books, movies, and word of mouth, each a magical effort to bind time and by this means, create magic, the transformation of the material world.

CHAPTER 27:

ANCIENT MAGIC

Magic is the most ancient of all art/sciences. It is the source of religion, theatre, yes, even and particularly stage magic or illusion. It is the source of mathematics, and all that follows there from. From the magical art of Alchemy arises chemistry, biology and pharmacology. The idea of cloning is predated by the ancient magical idea of homunculi. From astrology comes astronomy. Magic is the source of writing – runes – and words of power. Yes, and wine as well. Hail Bacchus! Magic is the source of psychology. Sorcery. And medicine, Shamanism. Some might argue with these claims, but they are true.

Still, while magic has been, and always will be, at the very edge of human (and other than human) invention, experimentation, and pioneering, the true work of magic is, and always will be, the perfection of the conscious being. This is the goal and purpose of elven magic, to help each and all develop "theirs'Elves" to complete perfection, so each of us can be as intelligent, powerful, healthy, beautiful, happy and creative as possible. All other endeavors are just sidelines, and benefits or bonuses, to the true purpose of magic.

There are those who would argue (and personally, we are absolutely sick of people who argue) that magic is a refuge for insecure people who wish to hide from the realities of life; and while it is true that magic does attract many weak and insecure individuals (who needs it more?), magic does not avoid reality but confronts it on all planes of being and existence. It is not we who are avoiding reality, in our view, but those who ignore the worlds and importance of spirit, soul, feeling, imagination and karma.

Magic is exciting, intriguing, mysterious and yes, sometimes dangerous, and one is advised not to involve ones'elf with it idly, or even deeply, without the courage and stamina it demands. Magic deals with the reality of the material world equally with that of the mental worlds, the emotional worlds, the worlds of spirits, and the realms of fantasy and dreams. There are few that involve thems'elves with magic for any length of time who do not prosper in some way because of it, and that includes those slimy con artists who involve thems'elves in magic only long enough to rush off and make money preaching about how Jesus saved them from their life of debauchery, Satanism and sin.

For those who "stay the course", there is the satisfaction that comes with personal triumph over one's own and other's demons, and the rewards that ultimately follow from having been true to one's own s'elf, and one's own dreams. While magic is open to everyone, we have found that only a few are open to it, which is only to say that, at this stage in evolution, there are few that have evolved to the point where they are ready to develop and use their own esoteric powers.

CHAPTER 28:

THE BODY AND MAGICK

I t is important that you learn to both live within this body as fully as possible and to direct this body so that it is successful in all things, and acts with integrity in all that it (one) does!

Sacrificing Your Virginity

Sex is meant to be special… to be magical. Particularly, one's first sexual experience should be a magical and memorable occasion. If you are participating in the ancient ceremony of the Sacrifice of One's Virgin-ity be sure to make this event as magical as possible. Need we say more?

Well, yes, we'll say a bit more. Sex should be wondrous. So should magic, particularly elven magic. To the elves, sex and magic are almost synonymous. Often one's first experiences or attempts at sex and/or magic are only memorable for one's lack of knowledge and experience and the clumsy, fumbling manner in which it takes place. However, if one perseveres and genuinely endeavors to improve one's technique, one is bound to get better at it. This is true of sex, magic and all other things. And in elfin magic particularly, always consider that elegance and beauty, kindness and understanding, patience and care, all go a long way in creating the proper atmosphere.

The Body of Light

One of the most important exercises for the magician-ess is to strengthen hir body of light, hir astral body. This is the body one uses when one is dreaming. It is also the body one uses when one is fantasizing about having sex with someone, or winning the lotto, or becoming a hero-ine, or whatever.

Most acts of magic are carried out in one's mind before one ever does anything on the material plane. In fact, it is the magic of the astral s'elf that set the material s'elf in motion. When you imagine what you will say to your boss to ask for a raise, or what you will say to an employee you have to fire or lay off, or what you will say to a date to get hir intrigued with you, these are all performances by your mental body attempting to locate the pathway to success and avoid the pit falls that lead to failure. If you add feeling to this you are adding the astral body. When you imagine all this, thought, feeling and sight, you enter the imaginal realm in which the body of light resides, the world of spirits.

It is important to do all one can to gain mastery over these bodies and merge them together as a whole, just as an actor seeks to gain perfect control over hir expressive s'elf, or a weight lifter over hir muscles.

When you die, which is to say shed your physical body, you will only have the integrated body of light to move about in. The greater your mastery of that body, the greater are your chances of finding a suitable replacement for your physical body when you need to do so. (At some point, one becomes truly adept in the use of that body and at that time some choose to abide in it permanently).

When the bodies are one, merged perfectly, you can react and act in life purely... naturally, and without forethought. When your body of light is perfected you can act with total confidence and certainty on the material plane, free from doubt and worry. In this way, all that you do succeeds. Every magician and magic wielder who strives to advance into the higher dimensions devotes hirs'elf to this end, which is becoming fully perfected in one's own true s'elf. This is the goal of the Elven Way, the Path of the Elfin that all Seelie Elves tread.

CHAPTER 29:

MISTAKES, DEMONS, AND THE

LOWER ASTRAL PLANES

I f we started over every time we made a minor mistake we'd never complete most rituals. Some magicians may strive for perfection every time, we elves strive to ever do our best and to make the most of what we've done.

Mistakes

It happens at times that a magician-ess may make a mistake during the performance of a magical ritual or ceremony. Quite often at these times the demons will begin chattering about the dread consequences of your error and how the magic will fail, etc. Simply ignore them. If you have made a mistake, correct it or incorporate it. Just as you would use your eraser or white out, or delete button or backspace, clear the mistake from you mind and do it right this time and proceed on. Simply start from the point before the error and then continue in the appropriate fashion, as though the mistake had never occurred. Dwelling on the error feeds the demons. The best way to deal with unwanted demons is to ignore them, give them no energy, and they will soon go elsewhere. The more energy you put into worrying about the mistake the greater it becomes.

It is true that the mistake may return as a blip in the magic, an obstacle, a slight derivation, but it will right itself as quickly as you did.

And remember in magick, particularly Elven Magic, intention is vital, for our magick stems from the more subtle realms and dimensions. In mundane chemistry if you put together chemicals in the right combination following the correct method the result will always be the same. It does not matter whether you are a good person, or a "bad" person, or whether your intentions are good or not. If you do the formula correctly the chemistry will work. Some folks believe magick works in the same way. That one must be scrupulously exact in one's workings. But Elven Magick stems from the Elfin/Faerie Dimensions where nothing is exact, everything is shifting, and imagination and intention are vital. In Elven Magick following a formula exactly is not anywhere near as important as having the proper attitude and intention. If your intention is clear, your assisting and attending spirits will clarify any technical errors (see Stein *Essential Reiki*). In dealing with demons, however, if you chose to do that, the letter of the agreement becomes vital. Nearly every demon fancies hirself a lawyer, and many are.

The Chattering Mind

At times, the demons refuse to shut up. They will manifest in the form of mind chatter. It is presupposed that you have calmed yours'elf sufficiently prior to the ceremony, and that this is, in fact, the appointed time. But still there are times when the demons seek to draw your attention away from what you are doing. Again, action and concentration are the keys. Do not stop for the demons. Do not struggle with the chattering. Continue on with the ritual/ceremony, giving it your full attention. In time, as the ceremony progresses you will find that the demons will tire if you have not feed them attention, and they will quiet down and go away. It is at this point that the power of the ceremony will increase, and the fervor toward exaltation will heighten in earnest.

It is this powerful feeling of ecstatic experience that is the force with which you will energize your magic and with it feed the spirits who will carry out your will on the etheric and material planes. The Elven spirits do not feed on blood, but on ecstasy.

Rising on the Planes

The very lowest of the astral planes is the realm of demons and guardians. However, while these beings are very fierce looking and can be quite noisy, they are for the most part harmless. Their job is really just to warn you off, scare you away, to weed out the timid and the lazy from going further. If you do not listen to them and simply proceed on your way, they will disappear.

The real demons and dangers of the astral planes are to be found on the higher levels. Every level has its own dangers. The realms of pleasure and success can be just as dangerous to the magician, even more so than the realms of terror, struggle, and failure. In fact, as painful as they are, the realms of despair often deepen one's soul, while the realms of success often steal one's soul like a thief in the night. Prudence and caution are always called for as one advances, particularly as one succeeds and gains in power.

CHAPTER 30:

THE EYE OF THE TAO IS IN

EVERYTHING.

Nature, within which magic operates, and by whose laws it is made possible, is a commingling of forces; some of which have affinity for each other, some that are neutral to each other, and some that oppose each other. All things that have affinity to each other are similar. This is the basis of sympathetic magic. All forces that oppose each other are related by their opposition, in each the other exists in the smallest degree at the point of contact between them. This is one of the principles of Taoist magic, which strives to attain mastery by achieving balance between the opposing forces. Only neutral forces are not related to each other, but since they don't oppose them either, they remain unaffected by them. Neutral forces are like a stick in a river, going wherever the eddies send them. This is the basis of Zen magic, a magic that follows the path of least resistance, and acts by non-action. It is related to the Tarot card 0 – The Fool.

Thus all things can affect all other things to which they are connected. This is the basis of magic. In sympathetic magic, you affect things through their natural affinity and likeness, their association and similarity, like follows like. In opposition, pushing or yielding creates movement. Reverse psychology is an example of this type of magic; Aikido, Judo and Jujitsu also operate on this principle. The opposite force is not directly resisted but channeled as the riverbed channels the power of the river. Neutral magic allows things to take their natural course without interference. The expression, "Give them enough rope to hang themselves," is an example of this type of magic. Often, particularly in the case of negative forces, it is best, if at all possible, not to oppose a force but to allow it to dissipate its energy as it tries to batter itself against a wall that is not there. The Seelie Elf is acquainted with each of these magics and makes use of them and blends them as need and purpose demand.

The laws of nature bring all things into a continuously renegotiated balance. Sympathetic magic is balanced by opposing forces. Both sympathetic magic, and opposition or channeling magic, are moderated by the power of the neutral magic that associates with each through non-resistance. It is the negotiating element.

In all magic that you do, it is good to remember the balance. If you do magic to acquire lots of money, it is important to remember to put in some magic for money's proper use and distribution. It is not simply a matter of acquiring it. It is vital to use it well, for if you accumulate a fortune but do not use it wisely and effectively, what good will it have done you?

If you are a military person, and you plan an attack, you need to also prepare for a retreat in case your attack fails and save back some support in case of success or failure. If you are going to get married, it is best to plan for your divorce. It's true that you don't plan to ever get divorced, but that's the problem exactly, isn't it? If you do attractive magic, you need also to do a magic to subtly repel or filter out those who are not appropriate for your needs and wishes. For magic, like advertising, broadcasts over a extended area attracting a wide variety of people, and just like people coming for a job interview many will come who are not suited for it or not up to the job. The exception to this is if you already know the person you want and direct your magic specifically, like a phone call, but then you had better be certain this is really the person you want, and that this person is the right one for you. We often get what we want only to discover it's not what we thought it was. So in all the magic you do, consider the balance. For if You do not, Nature will.

CHAPTER 31:

YOUR HOLY GUARDIAN ANGEL

T here are several ways to view the idea of a Holy
Guardian Angel. The basic Christian idea is that
each human is so important to God that He
assigns an angel to spend all his time looking after that
individual. We find this egocentric view somewhat ludicrous,
but the idea that there are spirits that can be called upon in
times of need is a good and valid one, and the idea that there
are spirits who have evolved farther along the path of evolution
and spiritual development who might help us seems not only
likely, but logical.

There are certain spirits surely that are more attuned to you
than others. Perhaps you remind them of when they were
young struggling magicians and have chosen to be your
mentors, and while they do not watch over your every second,
they are available to assist you when implored to do so. (see our
book *An Elven Book of Spirits: Evoking the Beneficent Powers of
Faerie* for a list of 360 spirits that can be called to assist you.)

The Holy Guardian Angel has also been used to designate one's
true inner s'elf, or higher s'elf, the s'elf in potential. By
becoming attuned with this spirit, you come to know who you
really are and what you are capable of achieving, your true
destiny as allotted by your essential being.

Once you become attuned with this higher s'elf, you no longer
waste your time trying to be what others expect you to be, or
trying to do and be what you are incapable of doing and being.
You know who you are and what you want, and you pursue it
with every once of effort and energy that you have. We could
call this the knowledge and conversation with your Holy
Guardian DNA-RNA, or the knowledge and conversation with

your true soulful potentiality, or the knowledge and conversation with your true S'elf.

While such a process is both valid and essential, it is important to remember that one's destiny and potential is often revealed in stages as one continues to progress on one's personal path and one's knowledge and capabilities increase, mature and develop. S'elf knowledge and initiation are not way-stations upon the road but the path itself. While the way-station can reveal part of the road ahead, it can never reveal it all. One is constantly learning what one's true capabilities are. The road is never ending, and there is always a part far ahead where the road blurs into the horizon and only by approaching it can its secrets be revealed to us.

The third aspect of the Holy Guardian Angel is the Angel as lover, the Faery Lover. Here your more perfected s'elf is also "your better half", your perfect lover. This is in accord with the many religions and beliefs that posit total union with the Godhead, the merging with the Divine. In this case, the Divine is seen as your lover with whom one must merge in order to become complete.

This idea is also related to the myth-legend-history that states that the Angels of God, the Annunaki, the Nephilim found the daughters of man pleasing and mated with them. This myth is also expressed in the story of Lillith - Avalae mating with Adam, and yes, Lucifer/Enki (that olde snake (druid/wizard-wise one) dallying with Eve. From these stories come the bastardized ideas of incubi, succubi, and vampires.

The ancient custom of letting the lord or king of the land mate with young virgins before her wedding, or on the wedding night, is also derived from this myth, for here the Divine king helps instill his greatness in the common people, thus uplifting them (theoretically). Groupies, and fans of movie/rock stars/sports figures/military heroes, who eagerly line up to be laid by their screen or music idol are another expression of this idea.

In all this is the notion that by being in touch with higher beings one can be uplifted. Thus comes the urge to possess things that have been owned by the famous, or to be in the places they have been, or that were a part of their being, relics (contagious magic). By touching what they have touched we become associated with them and absorb some of the magic they left behind. Quantum Theory suggests this is literally true.

We could say that all this is the design of our genetic inclinations – DNA/RNA seeking to merge/have intercourse with another being in order to create an ever more perfected s'elf. It is no accident, but rather the design of Nature that the beautiful, the intelligent, the rich, successful, and famous are given more opportunities for intercourse than those less fortunate. For all these traits, including a tendency toward longevity, are all preferred genetic factors, which is to say nearly all of us would prefer to be beautiful, rich, successful, etc. In pursuing those preferences, we shape the race toward greater success, beauty and genetically preferred features. Our angels, guardians, our genetic programming, all guide us toward being, merging and creating more beautiful, intelligent, creative, long living and successful s'elves. It is what we are here to do.

CHAPTER 32:

HOMUNCULUS

For centuries, magicians have attempted to create human life by artificial means. This endeavor has been looked at as everything from ridiculous to absolutely evil (read *The Magician* by W. Somerset Maugham based loosely upon Aleister Crowley). Now this endeavor is called cloning and genetic engineering, and while it has not totally gained acceptance, it is no longer thought ridiculous, although there are still those who feel it to be evil.

The object of this endeavor has generally been of two types: 1. To create more perfect human beings. And 2. To create perfectly willing worker slaves. The first motivation partakes of the Great Work. The second, to create slaves, the object of zombie-ism (see the movie *The Serpent and the Rainbow*), is now directed to a field we call robotics and unfortunately often partakes of the strivings of the Dominance Clique.

Magic has been and is always on the cutting edge of "human" pioneering. The magical ideas of the past, which seemed ridiculous at that time, are now the cutting edge of modern scientific explorations. The seemingly ridiculous ideas of the magic of today will be the science of tomorrow. We Seelie Elves are not against scientific research, however, we are always in favor of it being done with integrity, and a deep and abiding concern for humanity, the planet Earth and all of life.

CHAPTER 33:

THE DEATH PENALTY

A
t the time of this writing, there is a continual debate in American Society about the Death Penalty. Many people want "an eye for an eye", while others question whether killing prevents murder. For many Christians, the death penalty would seem a perfect punishment since it would immediately send the evil doer to face God and then on to hell.

However, if you believe in reincarnation, the death penalty would simply release the killer to go find another life, and most likely, due to the laws of Karma, once again face the issues and forces that lead to their murderous activities in the first place. Under those circumstances it would seem wise not to execute killers but to find a true program designed to rehabilitate them. Not that we could ever release them, for in most cases that would be tragically unwise, but we must remember death will eventually release them anyway, and we elves find we must think not only of the present but of the future.

It is true that rehabilitation will have little effect if the individual is subjected to the same insane and cruel pressures and treatment when it reincarnates as a child again, but perhaps if we could bring ours'elves to stop using prisons as houses of torment and torture, we would in part start to stem the tide of insane and callous cruelty that produces so many killers in society. The choice of the Seelie Elf, living in the world of men, is always: are we doing the most intelligent and loving thing that can be done? Are we improving the intelligence of society, or stifling it?

CHAPTER 34:

ENKI/LUCIFER REMEMBERED?

When we saw Enki, we recognized him immediately. We knew who he was, and in that moment we also remembered who we are, and the vow we'd swore together eons ago to free intelligence from the bonds of ignorance, to rid the soul of the chains of repression, to liberate the body from the grip of death, and to awaken our spirits from the slumber of hopelessness.

Do you remember us? Do you remember the oath we swore together to roam Time/Space until all our kindred were freed? No matter where you are. No matter how long it takes. We will find you and bring to you the song of freedom that echoes in our hearts.

Enki smiled at us, no, grinned at us, and without his saying a word it all came back to us ... lifetime after lifetime we have been on this sacred quest, and in lifetimes still to come it will continue. And each in hir own time shall be reminded of hir own vow, and the dreams sHe had as a child, and what seemed lost forever will be found to have merely strayed for a while. Welcome, elfin, we are on our way home.

CHAPTER 35:

THE GREAT WORK

What is the Great Work? The Great Work is the perfection of creation. To perfect ours'elves in each and every detail is the true work of humanity, of which a great many (but not all) of we elves have devoted ours'elves. To become the most intelligent, beautiful, creative, successful, immortal, and happy beings we can be is the Great Work. To fulfill our individual s'elves to the utmost extent, and indeed, to constantly expand our power and potential, is the Great Work of Humanity, and of we Seelie Elves who seek to uplift all of creation.

By doing everything the best we can, by living each moment to the best of our ability, we unite in action with our most divine inner being, our perfected s'elf. We become the expression of the divine manifest on Earth. We awaken to our angelic (radiant) elfin s'elfhood, and shake off the dreamless sleep caused by repression, and enforced by fear and guilt.

The Great Work is to help each of us be the most effective and productive we can be in a way that is healing and regenerating. The Great Work is the work of creating a Masterpiece of Living. The Art of Living with grace and beauty, intelligence and love, compassion, kindness and courtesy, and a great deal of style, we call Faerie Art. It is the true creative art of the elves.

ABOUT THE AUTHORS

The Silver Elves, Zardoa and Silver Flame, are a family of elves who have been living and sharing the Elven Way since 1975. They are the authors of *The Book of Elven Runes: A Passage Into Faerie; The Magical Elven Love Letters, volume 1, 2, and 3; An Elfin Book of Spirits: Evoking the Beneficent Powers of Faerie; Caressed by an Elfin Breeze: The Poems of Zardoa Silverstar; Eldafaryn: True Tales of Magic from the Lives of the Silver Elves; Arvyndase (Silverspeech): A Short Course in the Magical Language of the Silver Elves; The Elven Book of Dreams: A Magical Oracle of Faerie; The Book of Elven Magick: The Philosophy and Enchantments of the Seelie Elves; What An Elf Would Do: A Magical Guide to the Manners and Etiquette of the Faerie Folk; Magic Talks: On Being a Correspondence Between the Silver Elves and the Elf Queen's Daughters; Sorcerers' Dialogues: Further Correspondence Between the Silver Elves and the Elf Queen's Daughters and The Elven Tree of Life Eternal: A Magical Quest for One's True S'Elf.*

We have had various articles published in *Circle Network News Magazine* and have now given out over 5,000 elven names to interested individuals in the Arvyndase language, with each elf name having a unique meaning specifically for that person. If you wish to know more about us you can read pages 100 to 107 in *Circles, Groves and Sanctuaries*, compiled by Dan and Pauline Campanelli (Llewellyn Publications, 1992), which contains an article by us and photos us and our home/sanctuary as it existed at the time. You can also find an article about us in volume 4 number3, issue # 15 of *Renaissance Magazine*. We are also mentioned numerous times in *Not In Kansas Anymore* by Christine Wicker (Harper San Francisco, 2005), and *A Field Guide to Otherkin* by Lupa (Megalithica Books, 2007).

The Elven Way is the spiritual Path of the Elves. It is not a religion. While all elves are free to pursue whatever spiritual path they desire, or not as the case may be, these elves are magicians and follow no particular religious dogma. We do however believe in all the Gods and Goddesses, (also Santa Claus [to whom we're related], the tooth fairy [distant cousins] and the Easter or Ostara Bunny [no relation].) and try to treat them all with due respect. The Elven Way promotes the principles of Fairness, that is to say both Justice, Elegance and Equal Opportunity and Courtesy that is respectful in its interactions and attitude toward all beings, great or small. We understand the world as a magical or miraculous phenomena, and that all beings, by pursuing their own true path, will become whomever they truly desire to be. Our path is that of Love and Magic and we share our way with all sincerely interested individuals.

We welcome you to contact us through our website at: http://silverelves.angelfire.com or through our Facebook page, under the name Michael J. Love (Zardoa of the SilverElves) and Martha Char Love (SilverFlame of the SIlverElves) and we will do our best to help you.

Made in the USA
Las Vegas, NV
06 December 2020

12192855R00144